Winners Circle

The
American Homebrewers Association's

Winners Circle

10 Years of Award-Winning Homebrew Recipes

 Brewers Publications
Boulder, Colorado

Editors
Tracy Loysen
Charlie Papazian
Marjie Raizman
Copyright © 1989 by the Association of Brewers Inc.

ISBN 0-937381-14-4
Printed in the United States of America
10 9 8 7 6

Compiled by the American Homebrewers Association

Illustrations and cover design by John Martin

Selected style definitions from *The Association of Brewers' Dictionary of Beer and Brewing* (Brewers Publications, 1988) by Carl Forget, used with permission.

Published by Brewers Publications, a division of the Association of Brewers Inc., PO Box 1679, Boulder, CO 80306-1679 USA, (303) 447-0816; FAX: (303) 447-2825.

Acknowledgements

We wish to thank the many hundreds of brewers and beer enthusiasts who have contributed their time and effort in staging, registering, judging, organizing and promoting the American Homebrewers Association's first ten years of National Homebrew Competitions. And we especially wish to express our appreciation to all those brewers who entered and contributed their recipes for all of us to learn from. All those years . . . all those beers.

Contents

What Is a Winner?

By Charlie Papazian

What does it take to be a winner? The answer in every case is to relax, don't worry and have a homebrew — usually your own because you know that the best homebrew in the world is the one you brewed.

Only homebrewers know the secret satisfactions of serving and enjoying their own beer. You don't have to win a competition to be a winner. That's the nice thing about this hobby.

The Winners Circle is a compendium of some very special homebrew recipes contrived by homebrewers whose beer above all else represents a level of expertise every homebrewer can take pride in. The recipes are selected winners from the American Homebrewers Association's first ten annual National Homebrew Competitions. This premier event has taken place each spring since 1979. Thousands of bottles of homebrew have been submitted from Australia, New Zealand, Germany, Canada and the United States to compete in 23 classes of lager and ale, and in two classes of honey mead.

The logistics of preparing for this event are mind-boggling, as it now takes more than 700 people-hours to register, prepare and judge the nearly 1,000 entries in our current competitions. This makes it the largest beer competition of any kind in the history of our planet.

During the competition's ten years the judging has drawn on the most qualified people in the brewing community. Both profes-

Entry No. _____ Round No. _____
Class _____ Subcategory _____
Judged By (please print) _____

Max. Score

BOUQUET/AROMA (as appropriate for style) 10 _____
Malt (5)
Hops (5)
Other Fermentation Characteristics

APPEARANCE (as appropriate for style) 10 _____
Color (4)
Clarity (3)
Head Retention (3)

FLAVOR (as appropriate for style) 15 _____
Malt (3)
Hops (3)
Balance (4)
Conditioning (3)
Aftertaste (2)

BODY (full or thin as appropriate for category) 5 _____

DRINKABILITY & OVERALL IMPRESSION 10 _____

TOTAL (50 possible points): _____

Scoring Guide: Excellent 40-50; Very Good 30-39; Good 25-29;
Drinkable 20-24; Problem <20.

COMMENTS

☐ Alcoholic   ☐ Astringent   ☐ Nutty
☐ Fruity/Estery   ☐ Sulfury   ☐ Salty
☐ Sour/Acidic   ☐ Husky/Grainy   ☐ Sweet
☐ Phenolic/Medicinal ☐ Metallic   ☐ DMS
☐ Diacetyl/Buttery   ☐ Light Struck (skunky)
☐ Oxidized/Stale (winey, cardboard, rotten pineapple)

Judges please note: write extended comments on reverse.

Bottle Inspection _____
Aroma _____
_____

Appearance _____
_____

Flavor _____
_____

Overall _____
_____

- Use other side for additional comments -

The AHA's scoresheet for evaluating entries. Scoresheets are returned to each contestant with extensive remarks by the judges.

sionals and amateurs have contributed their time and expertise over the years, enabling the AHA's National Homebrew Competition to excel in the service and educational value it offers to the contestants and to homebrewers everywhere.

There are several reasons that the AHA National Competition has enjoyed success and the continued participation of homebrewers throughout the world. First, of course, there are winners chosen in each of the beer and mead categories. These winners represent personal excellence indeed, but more importantly their brews represent the excellence and quality our hobby has achieved. The beers in *The Winners Circle* are reflected in each and every one of our own brews.

Secondly, competitions broaden everyone's knowledge about beer and brewing. They serve as a reason to learn how to evaluate beer. The judges' evaluations help others improve their beer, and in the case of American homebrew competition judgings, the level of expertise of many judges is so high that their evaluations are worthy of consideration by commercial brewers. This is especially true of those judges participating in the American Homebrewers Association and the Home Wine and Beer Trade Association's National Beer Judge Certification Program.

Thirdly, competitions add an educational dimension for all those involved — the organizer, the judges and the entrants. There are no losers in a well-run homebrew competition. When judging is done with integrity and with standards developed by the entire homebrewing community, every brewer can learn something from the evaluations that are returned to him or her; why beer tastes the way it does, good or not so good.

Over the past ten years of the National Competition nearly 4,000 entries have been judged. There have been some very exciting moments for the winners, many of whom have pursued their brewing interests by opening their own small breweries or by becoming professional brewmasters. But most have remained perfectly content continuing to homebrew, tinkering with recipes and techniques for their personal homebrews.

The 126 recipes in this book represent tens of thousands of hours of fine tuning, experimentation, evaluation and decision making. They are a measure of the quality of the millions of batches of beer homebrewed in America today.

The Best of the Winners:
The Homebrewer of the Year

The American Homebrewers Association's
National Homebrew Competition, 1979-1988

1979　Tim Mead, Boulder, Colo.
　　　　Unusual, *Rag Time Black*
1980　Mary Beth Millard, Turner, Ore.
　　　　Light Lager, *Birthday Brew Snow-High Light Lager*
1981　Dave Miller, St. Louis, Mo.
　　　　Light Lager, *Dutch Style Lager*
1982　Donald Thompson, Dallas, Texas
　　　　Light-Bodied Light Lager
1983　Nancy Vineyard, Santa Rosa, Calif.
　　　　All-Grain Light Beer, *American Steam*
1984　Dewayne Lee Saxton, Chico. Calif.
　　　　Wheat Beer, *Du Bru Ale*
1985　Russell Schehrer, Boulder, Colo.
　　　　Porter, *Toluene Porter*
1986　Byron Burch, Santa Rosa, Calif.
　　　　Strong Beer, *Jerry Lee Lewis*
1987　Ray Spangler, Erlanger, Ky.
　　　　Saison, *Toadex Bloatarian Ale*
1988　John Maier, Juneau, Alaska
　　　　Barley Wine, *Oregon Special*

Meadmaker of the Year

1981　Roger Haynes, Thousand Oaks, Calif.
　　　　Barkshack Gingermead No. 12
1982　Ben Edmundson, Memphis, Tenn.
1983　Robert Townley, Westminster, Colo.
　　　　Raspberry Lemon Grass Ginger Mead
1984　Earl Koster, Westminster, Colo.
　　　　Raspberry Lemon Grass Ginger Mead
1985　Bill Pfeiffer, Wyandotte, Mich.
　　　　Black Raspberry Mead
1986　John Montgomery, Bryan, Texas
　　　　Reisling Pyment 64D
1987　Kerry Carpenter, Baker, Ore.
　　　　Royal Anne Gingermead
1988　Ralph Bucca, District Heights, Md.
　　　　Morat

Selection of the Recipes

The recipes in this compendium were chosen from many hundreds of first, second and third place winners. To the extent possible, we have selected malt extract, combination mash-malt extract (mash-extract) and all-grain recipes from each class and subcategory of styles open to competition in the Nationals.

The presentation of these recipes has been carefully designed so that they will be both useful and understandable to brewers of all levels of expertise. This book is for beginners in search of their first recipes, for intermediate brewers wishing to add to their repertoire of styles, and for advanced brewers fine-tuning a recipe.

Organization of Recipes

In order to facilitate its usefulness, the book is divided into three sections: Ale, Lager and Mead. The main classes or styles of these three sections are listed in alphabetical order. Some classes of beers can be further subcategorized. For example, the subcategories in the main Pale Ale class are India Pale Ale, Classic Pale Ale and British Bitter. These subcategories also are listed in alphabetical order.

The recipes are presented under their appropriate class and subcategory in a specific order useful for those who enjoy quickly referencing recipes based on level of complexity. Whenever possible, the first recipes are malt-extract based, followed by mash-extract techniques. The last recipes in any given section are all-grain recipes.

As much useful information as possible is included with each recipe entry. In addition to the list of ingredients and the batch size of each winning beer we have also included "brewer's specifics" whenever the brewer supplied this information with the recipe registration form. Of particular interest to anyone using these recipes is a short summary of judges' comments. In many instances this is invaluable information for fine-tuning a recipe to your own taste preferences.

Just as there are thousands of truly winning homebrew recipes, there are thousands of techniques capable of producing them. We know for a fact that many of the winners brewed with simple, unsophisticated, plastic bucket fermenters kept underneath their kitchen tables. At the other extreme were brewers who had the resources to brew with stainless-steel fermenters in temperature-controlled environments.

The beauty of all these recipes is that most of them can be used with whatever kind of equipment and technique you are using. Perhaps the only technique that all of them use, and undoubtedly the most important technique, is that of cleanliness and sanitation in the homebrewery. The best and easiest recipes in the world can be laid to ruin by poor sanitation techniques.

With regard to brewing techniques, we refer readers to their local homebrew supply shop for the many excellent books available on this subject.

Use this book as a tool in developing your own skills as a brewer. Perhaps someday we will have the pleasure of also recognizing your achievements in the winners circle.

And remember, worrying can spoil the taste of homebrew more than anything else in the world. So relax and have a homebrew and enjoy the world of brewing.

ALT

German Altbier.
A traditional style
of beer brewing found
mainly in Düsseldorf but also in Münster, Korschenbroich,
Krefeld, Issum and a few other cities of Northern Rhineland
and Westphalia. The German word *alt* means old or ancient
and refers to the fact that these beers are brewed by the
traditional method of top fermentation. This predates the
relatively new method of bottom fermentation introduced in
the mid-18th century and now predominant throughout
Germany.

Alt beers have a deep, luminous, copper color. They are brewed from dark malts, are well hopped and display a slightly fruity, bittersweet flavor. Their alcohol content varies from 3.5 to 4.0 percent by weight (4.4 to 5.0 percent by volume), and they are brewed from an original gravity of about 1.050 (12.5 degrees Balling). Those from Düsseldorf have Echte Düsseldorfer Altbier written on the label.

Kölsch. A very pale, golden-hued, top-fermented beer produced in the metropolitan area of Bonn-Cologne. Under German law, when Kölsch is brewed elsewhere in Germany, the name of the locality must precede the word. Kölsch is highly hopped, mildly alcoholic (3.7 percent by weight, 4.6 percent by volume) and slightly lactic in taste.

Etym: From Köln, the German name for the city of Cologne. Kölschbier is beer from that city.

League City Alt

Steve Daniel
League City, Texas
First place, Alt, 1988
(extract recipe)
(German Altbier)

Ingredients for 5 gallons
7 1/2   pounds Brewmaster light unhopped malt extract
   2   ounces crystal malt
   1   ounce Perle hops (60 minutes)
   1   ounce Perle hops (10 minutes)
1/2   ounce Perle hops (end of boil)
      Home-cultured W-338 alt beer yeast
      Forced CO_2 to prime

- Original specific gravity: 1.050
- Terminal specific gravity: 1.016
- Age when judged (since bottling): 3 months

Judges' comments

"Aroma very malty, caramel, no hop nose, no off-aromas. Nice amber color but a little light for style. Caramel sweetness, smooth, then bitter bite comes through. This has a little butter/diacetyl taste. You may have racked and cooled this too quickly, separating it from its yeast before it was ready. Overall this is a good beer, well made with plenty of drinkability. Add a few dark grains and your beer will be perfect in color."

"Very clean aroma. Good amber color. Good head retention and clarity. This is what an alt beer should taste like. Could drink this all day long."

Anchor's Away Alt Beer

Clark Swisher
Sacramento, California
First Place, Alt, 1987
(all-grain recipe)
(German altbier)

Ingredients for 5 gallons

    7   pounds 2-row malted barley
    1   pound English crystal malt
  1/2   pound dextrine malt
  1/2   pound flaked barley
  1/2   pound wheat malt
    2   ounces chocolate malt
    1   teaspoon Irish moss (15 minutes)
    2   teaspoons gypsum (1 teaspoon in mash, 1 in lauter)
    2   ounces Cluster leaf hops (60 minutes)
    1   ounce Willamette leaf hops (60 minutes)
    1   ounce Cascade pellet hops (5 minutes)
    4   ounces slurry of Anchor Brewing Co. ale yeast into 3/4
        pint (1.035) yeast starter solution
  3/4   cups dextrose to prime

- Original specific gravity: 1.040
- Terminal specific gravity: 1.008
- Age when judged (since bottling): 2 months

Brewer's specifics
Mashed at 144 degrees F for 60 minutes (simple infusion mash).
Lauter at 176 degrees F for 25 minutes.

Judges' comments
"Aroma has good soft malt tones with just enough hops.
Fruitiness emerges with charm. The appearance of this ale invites
the eye to raise a glassful. Soft fruity flavor, good sweet malt
smoothness with enough robust hop character in the finish. Really
good smooth, light brew with dry satisfying hop finish."
"Excellent aroma, fine hopping and malt. Good color and nice
thick head. Fine hopping and balance. Has a slight astringent
aftertaste and slight grainy taste. Very fine beer — good in
category."

Untitled
Chas and Helen Murphy
Sacramento, California
Second Place, Alt, 1987
(all-grain recipe)

Ingredients for 6 gallons
    10 pounds 2-row malted barley
     2 pounds wheat malt
    12 ounces crystal malt
    10 ounces Munich malt
     4 ounces chocolate malt
   3/8 ounce Northern Brewer hop pellets (60 minutes)
   1/4 ounce Cascade hop pellets (60 minutes)
   1/8 ounce Chinook hop pellets (60 minutes)
   3/8 ounce Northern Brewer hop pellets (30 minutes)
   1/4 ounce Cascade hop pellets (30 minutes)
   1/8 ounce Chinook hop pellets (30 minutes)
     1 ounce Cascade hop pellets (20 minutes steep after boil)
     1 ounce Fuggles hop pellets (20 minutes steep after boil)

  2 tablespoons gypsum
1/4 teaspoon salt
  1 tablespoon Irish moss
  2 packages Muntona yeast
  1 cup dextrose to prime

- Original specific gravity: 1.052
- Terminal specific gravity: 1.015
- Age when judged (since bottling): 1 1/2 months

Brewer's specifics
    Mashed all grains with 3 1/2 gallons water and 1 tablespoon gypsum at 150 degrees F for 65 minutes. Sparged with 7 gallons water at 165 degrees F and 1 tablespoon gypsum for 20 minutes.

Beim Dom
Keith Dorschner
Greenleaf, Idaho
Second Place, Alt, 1988
(Kölsch style)
(all-grain recipe)

Ingredients for 5 1/2 gallons
  6 pounds pre-ground malt
1/2 pound barley flakes
1/4 pound crystal malt
1/3 ounce Perle hops (75 minutes)
  1 ounce Hallertauer hops (45 minutes)
  1 ounce Hallertauer hops (15 minutes)
1/2 ounce Hallertauer hops (dry hop)
1/2 teaspoon Irish moss (last 15 minutes)
  1 teaspoon water crystals (a blend of gypsum, epsom salt and NaCl)
  1 packet Edme ale yeast
  1 cup corn sugar

- Original specific gravity: 1.032
- Terminal specific gravity: 1.011
- Age when judged (since bottling): 3 months

Brewer's specifics
Strike water at 186 degrees F. Thin mash, initial temperature 152 degrees F. One hour mash. Lager at 38 degrees F for 2 months.

Judges' comments
"Faint maltiness, clean aroma. Perfect clarity and color for a Kölsch. Head looks like whipped cream. Smoothness, creaminess and bitterness come through nicely. A slight saltiness; may be too much. You've made a wonderful example of this beer style."
"Fresh, clean aroma. Too pretty. Soft, clear finish. Lacks distinction, also lacks *any* defects. Pass Go, collect $200. A fine beer. I can almost smell the Rhine."

Fun Gornisht Kölsch
Jeff Sternfeld
Santa Rosa, California
Third Place, Alt, 1988
(all-grain recipe)
(Kölsch)

Ingredients for 5 gallons
    6 pounds 2-row Klages malt
    1 pound Munich malt
 1/2 pound wheat malt
 1/4 ounce Cascade hops (60 minutes)
 1/4 ounce Chinook hops (60 minutes)
 1/2 ounce Cascade hops (30 minutes)
 1/4 ounce Chinook hops (30 minutes)
 1/4 ounce Hallertauer hops (30 minutes)
 1/2 ounce Cascade hops (2 minutes)
 1/8 ounce Hallertauer hops (2 minutes)

1/2 ounce Cascade hops (dry hop)
1 teaspoon gypsum
15 grams Whitbread ale yeast
5 ounces dextrose to prime

• Original specific gravity: 1.042
• Terminal specific gravity: 1.008
• Age when judged (since bottling): 1 1/2 months

Brewer's specifics
Add grains to 1 3/4 gallons water (with 1 teaspoon gypsum added) at 130 degrees F. Rest 30 minutes at 120 to 122 degrees F. Add one gallon water at 200 degrees F to raise mash temperature to 158 degrees F. Rest 60 minutes (adding heat when needed). Sparge with 3 1/2 gallons water at 177 degrees F. Collect 6 gallons wort. Add 1/2 gallon water to pot.

Judges' comments
"Light soft malt aroma with a touch of hops and fruitiness. Inviting, deep golden color. Perhaps even a bit too dark for Kölsch. Really smooth taste, good malt. Hops are big for the delicate nature of this beer; maybe lighter would be better. Very good beer. Your next effort should prove a killer! Keep up the good work."

"Wonderful hoppy aroma, a bit spicy, great for style. Great color, beautiful head. Flavor somewhat dry and bitter, appropriate to style. Good body, complex hops. Wunderbar!"

BARLEY WINE

Barley Wine. In England, the name given to any top-fermented beer of unusually high, wine-like, alcohol content prepared from worts of 1.065 to 1.120 (16 to 30 degrees Balling) original gravity yielding about 6 percent to 12 percent alcohol by volume. Barley wines are usually copper-colored or dark brown, strongly flavored, fruity and bitter-sweet, and are sometimes fermented with wine or Champagne yeast. Because of their unusual strength they often have little head retention and require long aging periods that range from six months to many years. They are often brewed for special events. Russian stout, although slightly less alcoholic (10.5 percent by volume), is classed by many as a barley wine while others consider it to be a style unto itself.

Barley Wine
Byron Burch and Nancy Vineyard
Santa Rosa, California
First Place, Sparkling Barley Wines, 1981
(extract recipe)

Ingredients for 12 1/2 gallons
        18 pounds John Bull hopped dark malt extract
    2 1/4 pounds John Bull plain light malt extract
         2 pounds crystal malt
         1 pound black patent malt (cracked)
        10 pounds corn sugar
         4 ounces Cluster pellets (for bitterness)
         3 ounces Bullion pellets (for bitterness)
    4 1/2 ounces Cascade pellets (for aroma)
   12 1/2 gallons water (soft)
             Champagne yeast
         2 cups corn sugar for priming
             Sweeten to taste with lactose at bottling

Holiday Ale
Russell Schehrer
Denver, Colorado
Second Place, Barley Wine, 1988
(mash/extract recipe)

Ingredients for 5 1/2 gallons
        11 pounds light dry malt extract
         2 pounds amber dry malt extract

  3   pounds two-row malt
  1   pound dextrine malt
  1   pound crystal malt
  1   pound Munich malt
1/2   pound six-row malt
5 1/2 ounces Bullion hops (60 minutes)
  1   ounce Hallertau hops (60 minutes)
  2   ounces Fuggles hops (30 minutes)
  2   ounces Goldings hops (30 minutes)
  2   ounces Tettnang hops (30 minutes)
1 2/3 ounces Fuggles hops (dry hop - primary)
1/2   teaspoon Irish Moss (last 5 minutes)
  1   teaspoon gypsum in boil
  2   packets Edme ale yeast
  1   ounce Epernay wine yeast
1/2   cup corn sugar

- Original specific gravity: 1.096 at 100 degrees F
- Terminal specific gravity: 1.016
- Age when judged (since bottling): 2 1/2 years

Brewer's specifics

Mash the crushed grains at 156 degrees for 1 hour. Add all Bullion and Hallertau hops after 1 hour. Add 2 ounces of Fuggles, all the Tettnang and all the Goldings after 1 1/2 hours. Add 1.6 ounces of Fuggles in the primary fermenter. (No blow-off method was used).

Judges' comments

"Nice, clean estery nose. It has a good, fine white head. Clear garnet color. Nice bead. A lovely, smooth vinosity. A complex brew. Great balance — nothing sticks out. An excellent barley wine."

"This beer has a nice aroma. It seems it could have a stronger nose. Color is a pretty, reddish tint. Nice, tiny bubbles. Good barley wine flavor. Good job. For barley wine connoisseurs, it hits the mark."

"Big intense, warming, alcoholic, fruity brew."

My Old Flame

Ray Spangler
Erlanger, Kentucky
Second Place, Barley Wine, 1988
(mash/extract recipe)

Ingredients for 5 gallons
- 8 pounds mild ale malt
- 5 pounds pale ale malt
- 1/2 pound toasted crystal malt
- 1/2 pound toasted Munich malt
- 5 ounces toasted pale ale malt
- 1/4 pound wheat malt
- 2 ounces Northern Brewer hops (60 minutes)
- 1 ounce Cascade hops (60 minutes)
- 1 1/2 ounces Tettnanger hops (40 minutes)
- 1 ounce Kent Golding hops (after boil)
- 1/2 ounce Cascade hops (after boil)
- Red Star ale yeast
- 8 ounces dry malt extract boiled with 1 quart wort to prime

- Original specific gravity: 1.081
- Terminal specific gravity: 1.030
- Age when judged (since bottling): 2 months

Judges' comments
"Fantastic aroma! Excellent blend and balance of hop-malt-esters. Appearance clean, clear and inviting. Flavor beautiful! Thick, slightly sweet, a little shy on bittering hops. I love this beer! A little more oomph from bittering hops next time!"

"Fruity aroma is evident—nice, but alcohol and hop character is lacking, though you have a nice-smelling beer. I'd say this is a terrific beer, though for Barley Wine it needs more assertiveness. Twenty percent more malt, 30 to 40 percent more hops (at least). Good strong 'Old Ale' type of Barley Wine."

Old Goat Barley Wine

Rich Chapin
Lincoln, Nebraska
First Place, Strong Beers,1985
(mash/extract recipe)

Ingredients for 3 gallons
      4 pounds pale malt
    2/3 pounds John Bull light extract
      1 pound crystal malt
      2 ounces black malt
      8 ounces brown sugar
      1 ounces Northern Brewer pellets (1 hour)
1 1/2 ounces Bullion pellets at boiling break
      1 ounces Fuggle pellets (5 minutes)
      1 tablespoon gypsum
      1 packet wine yeast
    1/2 cup corn sugar to prime

- Original specific gravity: 1.097
- Terminal specific gravity: 1.036
- Age when judged (since bottling): 9 1/2 months

Brewer's specifics
      Infusion mash in picnic cooler at 155 degrees F for 1 hour (strike water was 178 degrees). Sparge with 170 degree water to collect 3 gallons.

Judges' comments
      "Creamy head with a delicate bouquet and an excellently balanced flavor. A flawless brew."
      "Good malt/hop balance in the flavor."

Oregon Special

John C. Maier
Juneau, Alaska
First Place, Barley Wine, 1988
(mash/extract recipe)

Ingredients for 5 gallons
    11 pounds Williams Australian dry malt extract
     3 pounds Klages malt
     5 ounces Nugget hops (45 minutes)
 1 1/2 ounces Willamette hops (10 minutes)
     8 ounces yeast starter of Sierra Nevada culture
   3/4 cup dextrose to prime

- Original specific gravity: 1.075
- Terminal specific gravity: 1.025
- Age when judged (since bottling): 23 months

Brewer's specifics
    Mash grains at 120 degrees F for 30 minutes. Raise heat to 130 degrees F. Infuse boiling water, raise to 152 degrees for 15 minutes. Raise heat to 158 degrees F for 10 minutes. Raise to 170 degrees F. Sparge with 2 gallons 170 degree water.

Judges' comments
    "Big, voluptuous malt with good hop bouquet for balance. Elegant and robust. Beautiful color, just a touch hazy, though not at all a problem. Just a bit underprimed. Head retention really wonderful. Old Foghorn-like (Anchor barley wine). Enormously balanced and ruggedly elegant. Outside of a touch of chill haze and a definite undercarbonation (unless we're talking Thomas Hardy) — great effort!"
    "Nice bouquet. Good powerful balance between malt and hops. Pretty red color. Nice tiny bubbles. Good balance. Nice smooth finish. Among the best. Keep up the good work. Try some extra finishing hops. On to best of show!"

Barley Wine

Marty Velas and Solange Brun
Van Nuys, California
First Place, Strong Beer, 1985
(all-grain recipe)

Ingredients for 5 gallons
25 pounds pale Klages 2-row malt
1/2 ounces Fuggle hops (1 hour)
1/2 ounces Fuggle hops (50 minutes)
1 ounces Kent Golding hops (30 minutes)
3 teaspoons $CaSO_4$ (gypsum)
15 milliliters Sierra Nevada ale yeast culture
1 1/4 cups corn sugar to prime

- Original specific gravity: 1.088
- Terminal specific gravity: 1.022
- Age when judged (since bottling): 1 year, 8 months

Brewer's specifics
Mash at 125 degrees F for 20 minutes; 154 for 60 minutes; 170 for 5 minutes. Double-stage fermentation in glass at 65 degrees F for 13 weeks.

Judges' comments
"Aroma and flavor are excellent, like a Chimay ale."

BELGIUM-STYLE SPECIALTY BEER

Flanders Brown Ale.
A style of ale from Belgium made in the traditional way with barley malts but with a slightly sour, dry, lactic character.
This quality, combined with some of the fruity, spicy complexity obtained by using unique yeast strains and warm fermentations, produces some unparalleled brews.

Trappist Ales. Any beer brewed in one of the six remaining brewing abbeys, five of which are in Belgium and one in The Netherlands. Trappist beers are top-fermented, deep-hued (amber or brown) and fairly strong, ranging from 5.7 to 12 percent alcohol by volume (4.6 to 9.6 percent by weight); they are fruity and often bittersweet; they are bottle-conditioned by priming and re-yeasting.

The origin of Trappist beers dates back to the Middle Ages when epidemics were spread by contaminated water. Monasteries located on the traveling route to pilgrimage areas provided travelers with food, shelter and a hygenic beverage free of pathologic microbes. There were many abbeys all over Europe; Germany alone accounted for close to 500. In Belgium, two orders brewed beer: the Benedictines and the Cistercians. After the Revolution, only the Trappists (Cistercians of strict observance) continued to brew beer. There are five brewing abbeys left in Belgium: Chimay, Orval, Rochefort, St. Sixtus and Westmalle.

Saison. An amber- or copper-colored top-fermented beer from France and the Walloon (French-speaking) section of Belgium. It was once brewed in the late spring (April-May) from a high gravity wort and drunk four to six months later. It is now available all year round. Saison is naturally conditioned in burgundy-shaped one-liter bottles. It has a fruity flavor and an alcohol content of about 4.5 percent alcohol by weight (5.6 percent by volume).

Goudenband

Michael Matucheski
Antigo, Wisconsin
First Place, Flanders Brown Ale, 1988
(all-grain recipe)

Ingredients for 5 1/2 gallons
    7 pounds wheat malt
    3 pounds pale malt
    2 pounds crystal malt

1 1/2 ounces Cascade hops (45 minutes)
1/2 ounce Tettnanger hops (15 minutes)
      Liefman's Goudenband yeast culture
1/2 gallon fresh wort (1.052) to prime

* Original specific gravity: 1.052
* Terminal specific gravity: 1.012
* Age when judged (since bottling): 2 months

Brewer's specifics

All grains were home-grown and malted; all hops were home-grown. Mashed at 153 degrees F for three hours. Sparged at 163 degrees F to collect 6 1/2 gallons. Boiled one hour with above hop additions. One-hour hot break in kettle, then run off. Cooled overnight at air temperature of 50 degrees F. Yeast pitched at 8 a.m. into oak rain barrel. Racked to paraffin-lined oak barrel after six days. Racked to glass after three months and back to oak three months later. Bottled four months after that with 1/2 gallon fresh wort to prime.

Judges' comments

"Complex aroma characteristic of the style. Very clear, dark burgundy color. Multifaceted style. Appealing, very similar to a mead, wonderful characteristics."

"Bouquet is perfect! To style, just like Rodenbach. Great appearance. Outstanding complex balance of flavors; fruit, sour, sweet, low hops. Could even be more sour. Please send recipe!"

Sex

Pierre Rajotte
Montreal, Quebec, Canada
First Place, Flanders Brown Ale, 1987
(all-grain recipe)

Ingredients for 5 gallons
6 2/3 pounds 2-row malted barley
1/2 pound crystal malt
3 ounces black patent malt

   3 ounces chocolate malt
   1 ounce Cascade hops (90 minutes)
 2/3 ounce Cascade hops (30 minutes)
 1/3 ounce Fuggles hops (10 minutes)
 1/2 ounce Fuggles hops (after boil)
   1 ounce Canadian ale yeast
 2 1/2 ounces dextrose to prime

* Original specific gravity: 1.040
* Terminal specific gravity: 1.015
* Age when judged (since bottling): 7 months

Brewer's specifics
   Upward infusion: Started at 124 degrees F for 3/4 hour. Raised to 154 degrees F. Held one hour. Raised to 170 degrees F and sparged with 170 degrees F water.

Judges' comments
   "Aroma mild, yet true to character. Lovely hues. Flavor has dry licorice flavor, light tartness. Good hops in finish and specialty malt flavor. Very true to character. Probably marketable."
   "Slightly roasty aroma with a hint of appropriate sourness. Lovely color, crystal clear, excellent head. Small, smooth bubbles. Flavor a little tart. Beautiful balance. Maybe the body and mouth feel is a little light. Good job."

Saint Douglas Ale
John Dolphin
East Douglas, Massachusetts
Second Place, Trappist Ale, 1987
(extract recipe)

Ingredients for 5 gallons
 6 2/3 pounds Munton and Fison Old Ale hopped malt
         extract syrup
 3 1/3 pounds Munton and Fison light malt extract syrup
   1   pound clover honey

cultured Chimay yeast
3/4 cup dextrose to prime

- Original specific gravity: 1.073
- Terminal specific gravity: 1.020
- Age when judged (since bottling): 8 months

Judges' comments
    "Estery nose started very clean but didn't last. Appearance unusually clear! A slight haze is common for this style. Respectable alcoholic content! Very nice balance. Flavor faded—should have more sweetness. Very good effort! With a little more residual sweetness this would have been excellent!"
    "Style requires a hoppier, more flowery aroma; smell is pleasing but not soft and smooth. Good full clean head; a tad dark in color for a Trappist Ale. Immediate impression is of yeast bite, a bitterness preventing my acknowledging the subtler flavors that are present. Has diacetyl and estery quality characteristic of style. Pretty beer. Sits well. Get rid of yeast bite; increase malt—try for fuller body and more hops (good beer)."

St. Egregious
Byron Burch
Santa Rosa, California
First Place, Trappist Ale, 1987
(mash/extract recipe)

Ingredients for 7 1/2 gallons (10 gallons originally)
    15 pounds Great Fermentations light dry malt extract
     5 pounds Great Fermentations amber dry malt extract
     3 pounds Munich malt
     2 pounds Klages malt
    1/4 pound crystal malt
     8 bottles homemade kriek lambic (added to fermenter)
    1 1/2 ounces Chinook leaf hops (60 minutes)
    1 1/4 ounces Eroica pellet hops (60 minutes)
    1/2 ounces Cascade leaf hops (60 minutes)

    4   ounces Nugget pellet hops (30 minutes)
    1   ounce Cascade leaf hops (30 minutes)
  1/4   ounce Eroica pellet hops (30 minutes)
    8   ounces Cascade pellet hops (dry hopped)
    2   ounces Styrian Goldings pellet hops (dry hopped)
    2   ounces East Kent Goldings pellet hops (dry hopped)
    1   ounce Spalt pellet hops (dry hopped)
    1   ounce Willamette pellet hops (dry hopped)
   20   grams Great Fermentations Prise de Mousse wine yeast
1 1/2   cups dextrose to prime

- Original specific gravity: 1.101
- Terminal specific gravity: not available
- Age when judged (since bottling): 1 1/2 months

Judges' comments
    "Nice estery nose, somewhat alcoholic. A pleasure to sniff! Slight haze common for this style—not inappropriate. Nice creamy feel in mouth, nice body, well balanced—slight "smoke" aftertaste. Very good effort! You did a nice job! Clarity improves with warming. Hop aroma lingered for a long, long time!"
    "Nice maltiness, good alcohol in the nose. Developed fresh hops aroma standing. Chill haze? Slightly burned flavor—watch scorching. Lacks balance—sweetness is not married to bitterness. Alcohol apparent, flavors not blended. Try hopping less. Nice dessert beer, but not for extensive drinking. More aging might blend flavors."

Toadex/Bloatarian Ale

Ray Spangler
Erlanger, Kentucky
First Place, Saison, Best of Show, 1987
(all-grain recipe)

Ingredients for 5 gallons
  9 1/2   pounds pale ale malt
  1 1/2   pounds Munich malt

3/4 pound crystal malt
1/2 pound wheat malt
Irish moss (end of boil)
2 ounces Hallertauer hops (60 minutes)
1 ounce Tettnanger hops (60 minutes)
3/4 ounce Hallertauer hops (5 minutes)
1/2 ounce Cascade hops (5 minutes)
cultured Chimay "Rouge" ale yeast
2 ounces light dry malt extract
2 ounces dextrose boiled with 1 quart wort to prime

- Original specific gravity: 1.062
- Terminal specific gravity: 1.020
- Age when judged (since bottling): 6 months

Brewer's specifics
Decoction mash: 1/3 mash raised to boil, added back raising mash to 105 degrees F, 1/3 mash raised to boil for 10 minutes, added back raising mash to 148 degress F, 1/3 mash raised to boil for 5 minutes, added back raising mash to 158 degrees F. Mash raised to 170 degrees F for 10 minutes. Note: use 10-minute rest between steps.

Judges' comments
"Aroma is fantastic! Excellent blend and balance of hop-malt-ester. Beautiful flavor! A little shy on bittering hops. I love this beer! A little more oomph from bittering hops next time."

"Good color, appropriate for category."

"Soft, malty aroma and complex estery character. Very much like Saison Silly of Belgium. Deep orange-brown to auburn. Very true to what I have experienced through the one import I have tasted."

"There is a ring around the collar indicating a bacterial colony. Smells quite alcoholic. This brew is complex, clean and well balanced — in spite of the ring in the bottle! Nice job."

BROWN ALE

Brown Ale. In Britain, a dark-colored top-fermented beer considered by many to be the bottled equivalent of mild ale, although it is somewhat sweeter and fuller bodied. Brown ales are lightly hopped and are flavored and colored with roasted and caramel malts. They are brewed with soft water from original wort gravities ranging from 1.035 to 1.050 (9 to 12.5 degrees Balling), resulting in an alcohol content of about

3.5 percent or more.   Brown ales are sometimes called "bottled mild."

English Mild. In Britain, a dark brown top-fermented beer, light to medium bodied, malty, sweet and lightly hopped, more or less contrasted by bitter ale. It is prepared from an original wort gravity of 1.030 to 1.036 (8 to 9 degrees Balling) and may be bottled or casked, but is best appreciated as a draft beer. It is served mainly in the East and West Midlands and the northwest of England.

Baskerville Brown Ale
W.C. Embrey Jr.
Bellvue, Colorado
Second Place, Brown Ale, 1987
(extract recipe)

Ingredients for 5 gallons
        6 pounds Williams American light malt extract syrup
        1 pound dark dry malt extract
        6 ounces chocolate malt
        4 ounces black patent malt
        4 ounces dark crystal malt
        4 ounces dextrin (cara-pils) malt
        1 ounce malto-dextrin
    1 1/4 ounces Canadian Kent Goldings leaf hops (boil 60
               minutes)
      1/4 ounce Galena leaf hops (boil 60 minutes)
      1/4 ounce Belgian Hallertau pellet hops (finish 15 minutes)
      1/4 ounce Cascade pellet hops (finish 15 minutes)
        1 package Edme yeast
      2/3 cup dextrose to prime

- Original specific gravity: Didn't check
- Terminal specific gravity: Didn't check
- Age when judged (since bottling): 2 3/4 months

Brewer's specifics
    Grains were steeped in 120 degree F water for five minutes,

then strained and rinsed with tap water. Bittering hops were added to this water and boiled one hour. Extracts and malto-dextrin were added and boiled 30 minutes. Finishing hops were added last 15 minutes.

Judges' comments
"Slightly hoppy and fruity aroma. Nice subtle malty odor. Nice deep reddish brown color, good clarity. Nice carbonation, smooth, sweet, no hop bitterness. Well-blended flavor, slightly sweet aftertaste."

"Wonderful aroma — alcoholic. Appearance right on for category. Flavor has more alcohol than typical for brown ale. Sharp hop bitterness — clean hop flavor. Very drinkable/enjoyable. Somewhat aggressive flavor for brown ale."

"Slight malty sweetness in aroma. Maybe more aromatic hops would be useful. Has slight oxidized odor. Very appropriate appearance. The flavor has a malty sweetness and the light hopping appropriate for the style. Slight cidery aftertaste with warming alcoholic afterglow. Maybe too high alcohol-wise for style. Good, clean, drinkable. Very appropriate for style. Good score for first beer out of the box. Going to be hard to beat."

Good Beer

David A. Lose
Sebastopol, California
First Place, Heavy Bodied Dark Brews, 1983
(Brown Ale)
(extract recipe)

Ingredients for 6 gallons
- 7 pounds British light malt extract
- 3 1/3 pounds John Bull unhopped dark extract
- 2 ounces Cluster hops
- 1 teaspoon non-iodized salt
- 1 teaspoon generic yeast nutrient
- Edme ale yeast
- 1 cup corn sugar

- Original specific gravity: 1.050
- Terminal specific gravity: 1.018
- Age when entered (since bottling): 6 months

Brewer's specifics
Boil extract, 3 gallons water, salt and hops for 1 hour. Pour into fermenter and add water to make 6 gallons total. Pitch yeast when below 75 degrees F. Add nutrient. Ferment 4 days in primary fermenter, then 2 days in secondary. Prime with 1 cup corn sugar and bottle.

Judges' comments
"Needs more hop aromatics and a less bitter finish."
"Great CO_2. Hops and malt flavors profile balanced just right."
"Seems underhopped; very nice malt/grain balance. Good brew!"
"Nice body. Maybe short in finish hop. Nice sweetness and aftertaste."

Old Familiar
Maribeth Hoyme
Boulder, Colorado
First Place, Black Brews, 1981
(Brown Ale)
(extract recipe)

Ingredients for 5 gallons
    4 pounds dark dried malt extract
    8 ounces crushed roasted barley
    8 ounces crushed crystal malt
    2 ounces Cascade hops for boiling
    2 ounces Cascade hops for finishing (bagged in cheese-
       cloth)
    2 pounds dark brown sugar
  1/2 teaspoon plain salt
  1/4 ounce sparkolloid
    4 ounces molasses (for bottling)
       dried lager yeast

- Original specific gravity: 1.045

Brewer's specifics

Boil the malts, barley, boiling hops, salt and sparkolloid for 45 minutes with 2 gallons of water. Then turn off the heat, add the finishing hops and let the wort cool for 30 minutes. Sparge into the primary and add the finishing hops as well as the brown sugar. Add enough water for 5 gallons. When the batch has cooled to room temperature pitch the yeast.

After primary fermentation is complete, the brew should be racked into a secondary fermenter and lagered at cellar temperatures for four months, then bottled with molasses for carbonation and aged for two more months.

Nightcap

Dan Kellogg
Sacramento, California
First Place, Brown Beer, 1984
(Brown Ale)
(mash/extract recipe)

Ingredients for 5 gallons

1	pound 2-row (Canadian) malted barley
4	ounces flaked barley
1 1/4	pounds crystal malt
1	pound flaked maize
6	ounces chocolate barley
2	ounces roasted barley
1	ounce black patent
4	pounds John Bull dark extract
4	pounds John Bull light extract
1/2	inch brewing licorice
1 3/4	teaspoons gypsum
1	ounce Bullion hops (boil)
1	ounce Cascade hops (boil)
1	ounce Fuggles hops (boil)
1/2	ounce Brewers Gold hops (boil)
1	ounce Brewers Gold hops (finish)

　　　1　ounce Fuggles hops (finish)
　　1/2　ounce Cascade hops (finish)
　　1/8　ounce Hallertauer (in secondary)
　　　2　packages Edme yeast
　　　3　ounces lactose (for bottling)
　　　1　teaspoon ascorbic acid (for bottling)
　　　1　cup corn sugar (for bottling)

- Original specific gravity: 1.052
- Terminal specific gravity: 1.016
- Age when judged (since bottling): 1 year and 20 days

Brewer's specifics
　　Mashing: 40 minutes at 125 to 135 degrees F, 10 minutes at 150 degrees F. Sparge with water at 165 degrees F.

Judges' comments
　　"Nice aroma, sweet smell, good balance of malt and hops. Flavor is sweet but good!"
　　"Excellent clarity and head retention. Slight aroma, needs more — possibly more finishing hops. Strong aftertaste."
　　"Great appearance and aroma — perhaps a tad hoppy — but malt is nowhere near lost. Interesting sweet taste with hop finish and aftertaste. This is a winner. A slight diacetyl (like Prior Double Dark, but not as noticeable) would really cap it off!"
　　"Very nicely balanced with aromatic hops but not overpowering. Taste and finish are slightly malty, but hops come through well on aftertaste. This is a very drinkable brew, on the heavy side of brown beers, close to a porter."

Dun Rite Simpler

Bob Wood
Colorado Springs, Colorado
First Place, Brown Ale, 1988
(all-grain recipe)

Ingredients for 6 1/2 gallons
　　11　pounds Klages malt (step mash)

   1 pound crystal malt (step mash)
   1 ounce Cascade hops (45 minutes)
3/4 ounce Bullion hops (45 minutes)
1/2 ounce Chinook hops (15 minutes)
1/2 ounce Cascade hops (in hop back)
   2 teaspoons $CaSO_4$ (gypsum) in sparge water
      M.eV. ale yeast No. 13
1/4 teaspoon dextrose in each bottle to prime

- Original specific gravity: 1.068
- Terminal specific gravity: 1.018
- Age when judged (since bottling): 1 1/2 months

Judges' comments
   "Hop nose comes through well. Very clear, fine color for category. Flavor has a fine balance of hops to malt. Very drinkable, good ale."
   "Well balanced hop and malt aroma. Very clear (brilliant), good color, well-balanced flavor. I really like this brown ale."

How Now Brown
Mark Kessenich
Madison, Wisconsin
First Place, Brown Ale, 1985
(all-grain recipe)

Ingredients for 5 gallons
      6 pounds Kewauskun 2-row malted barley
      6 pounds Briess 6-row malted barley
      1 pound caramel malt
   1/2 pound chocolate malt
   1/2 pound stove-top roasted malt
      1 cup whole barley
      1 cup short-grain brown rice
      1 cup sweet brown rice
1 1/4 ounces Willamette (5.5 percent) hops (1 hour)
   1/4 ounce Northern Brewer (8 percent) hops (1 hour)

1/4   ounce Willamette hops (10 minutes)
1/4   ounce Northern Brewer hops (end of boil)
      Red Star ale yeast
2/3   cup corn sugar to prime

- Original specific gravity: 1.054
- Terminal specific gravity: 1.018
- Double-stage fermentation in hard plastic polycarbonate carboy, then stainless steel soda keg at 68 degrees F for 7 days.
- Age when judged (since bottling): 6 weeks

Brewer's specifics

Mash the malted barleys and cooked barley and rices for 35 minutes at 117 degrees F, 40 minutes at 135, 20 minutes at 153. Add the roasted malts and bring to 158 degrees for 50 minutes. Sparge with water at 177 degrees F (in plastic bucket with 1-inch holes and nylon screen).

Judges' comments

"Color is a bit dark for the category. Complex bouquet with a good balance — nice malt aroma with roast undertones and a good balance in the flavor. An excellent beer."

Dark Ale

Robert Carter
Watsonville, California
Second Place, Brown Ale, 1988
(English Mild)
(all-grain recipe)

Ingredients for 5 gallons
8   pounds Klages malt
1   pound Munich malt
1   pound crystal malt
1/4   pound chocolate malt
1/2   ounce Galena hops (60 minutes)
1   ounce East Kent Golding hops (15 minutes)

Brewer's Choice German lager liquid yeast
1/2 cup corn sugar

- Original specific gravity: 1.050
- Terminal specific gravity: 1.015
- Age when judged (since bottling): 2 months.

Brewer's specifics
Mash in at 122 degrees F and rest for 30 minutes. Raise to 155 degrees F and maintain for 60 minutes. Raise to 170 degrees F, sparge with 165 degree F water. Boil wort with Galena hops, whirlpool, let sit for 30 minutes. Run through heat exchanger and pitch yeast.

Judges' comments
"Good balance of hops and malt for the category. Very good, clean appearance. Excellent head retention. Well balanced flavor with a slight astringent taste, probably from grain tannins. A very well-brewed ale. I like this one."
"Malty aroma — true for category. Good, sharp color. Fine head. Nice malty flavor — not too much hop flavor. Very drinkable. I think I can taste a little chocolate malt."

CREAM ALE

Cream Ale. An American term for a mild, pale, light-bodied ale, around 4.75 percent alcohol by volume. Cream Ales are often made by blending an ale and a lager.

Australian Cream
Michael Stackpool
Denver, Colorado
Second Place, Cream Ale, 1987
(extract recipe)

Ingredients for 5 gallons
  6 pounds Brewmaster Australian malt extract syrup
1 1/2 ounces Cluster leaf hops
  1/2 ounce Hallertauer leaf hops
  1/4 ounce Hallertauer leaf hops
  2 packages Muntona yeast
  5 ounces dextrose to prime

- Original specific gravity: 1.037-1.040
- Terminal specific gravity: not measured
- Age when judged (since bottling): 2 1/2 months

Brewer's specifics
   Boil Cluster hops for a total of 60 minutes. Boil 1/2 ounce Hallertauer hops for 5 minutes. Remove from heat, add additional 1/4 ounce Hallertauer hops and steep for 20 minutes.

Judges' comments
   "Malty aroma, could use some more finish hops. Fairly clear appearance. Has a slight chill haze. Very good on the blend of hops to malt. Pleasant cream ale."
   "Aroma doesn't reach out much. Clean. A bit yeasty in a nice way. Appearance is a tad cloudy. Probably chill haze. Flavor is a bit too malty and bitter for the category but the beer tastes well brewed. Hopped on the spicy side. This beer needs to be served cold."
   "Good bouquet—mild hoppiness. Clear, good color, excellent head retention. Flavor excellent, mild. No harsh aftertastes, very clean. Excellent mouth feel—creamy, with great carbonation. This is *great* beer!"

Cotati Cream Ale

Paddy Giffen
Cotati, California
First Place, Cream Ale, 1987
(mash/extract recipe)

Ingredients for 5 gallons
- 5 pounds Klages malt
- 2 pounds wheat malt
- 2 pounds bulk light malt extract
- 1/2 ounce Saaz hops (60 minutes)
- 1/2 ounce Cascade hops (60 minutes)
- 1/2 ounce Saaz hops (30 minutes)
- 1/4 ounce Cascade hops (steep 15 minutes)
- 2 packages Red Star yeast
- 7/8 cup dextrose

- Original specific gravity: 1.040
- Terminal specific gravity: 1.011
- Age when judged (since bottling): 4 months

Judges' comments
"Aroma hoppy and very fresh. Appearance is excellent. Great head and retention. Flavor is full, smooth, mild. Great mouth feel, very mild aftertaste. Excellent beer, creamy, good hop aroma."

"Aroma makes a great first impression, malt comes through, then hops. Great effervescence. Flavor gives a lager-style impression, good mouth feel, hop bitterness masks malt finish a little."

Pride of Waseca

John G. Schmidt
Rohnert Park, California
First Place, Cream Ale, 1988
(all-grain recipe)

Ingredients for 5 gallons
- 6 pounds Klages malt

    1   pound light Munich malt
  1/2   pound wheat malt
  1/2   ounce Cascade hop pellets (60 minutes)
  1/2   ounce Cascade hop pellets (30 minutes)
    1   ounce Hallertauer hop pellets (30 minutes)
  1/2   ounce Chinook hop pellets (dry hopped)
    1   teaspoon gypsum
    1   package Brewers Choice German Lager liquid yeast
  3/4   cup dextrose to prime

- Original specific gravity: 1.042
- Terminal specific gravity: unknown
- Age when judged (since bottling): 3 months

Judges' comments

"Aroma very hoppy with a hint of malt. Nice golden color, clarity and carbonation. Flavor has an excellent hoppiness with a good malt background. Only drawback is the drop in intensity in the mid-mouth."

"Perfect 'green' hoppy nose, slightly light on the malt, but OK. Slight sulfury aroma. Beautifully clear. Nice head retention. Would be dark for a commercially brewed example. Flavor pretty clean, but slightly oxidized. Lingering astringent hop flavor. High carbonate water? Good effort at an extremely difficult style. I could drink a lot of this beer."

FRUIT BEER

Fruit Beer. Any ale or lager using fruit as an adjunct. The fruit may be added to the primary fermentation or later to produce a separate secondary fermentation. The particular fruit qualities of the beer should be distinct, yet harmonious with the total flavor profile.

Jake and Elwood's
Blueberry Lager

Fred LeVere
Des Moines, Iowa
Second Place, Fruit Beer, 1987
(extract recipe)

Ingredients for 4 gallons
3 1/3 pounds Laaglander light lager hopped malt extract syrup
1/2 pound Laaglander light dry malt extract
1 pound clover honey
4 pounds blueberries (steeped 20 minutes after boil)
1/4 ounce Hallertauer hop pellets (dry hopped in secondary)
1/4 ounce Cascade hop pellets (dry hopped in secondary)
2 packages Laaglander lager yeast
1/2 cup dextrose to prime

• Original specific gravity: unknown
• Terminal specific gravity: unknown
• Age when judged (since bottling): 4 months

Judges' comments
"Wow! What a great blueberry smell, like pie! Excellent color, deep blue purple, like pie. If anything a bit bitter, but not a fault. This is the best beer I've judged this year. I think it is best of show material!"

"Wow, what an aroma! Usually you can hardly smell blueberries. The color is wonderful and crystalline, the head nice. This was exquisitely brewed. Well balanced and clean. Keep up the good work."

Raspberry II
Martin Jolley
Gladstone, Missouri
First Place, Specialty Beers, 1985
(extract recipe)

Ingredients for 15 gallons
9 7/8   pounds John Bull light extract
10 1/16   pounds Edme dry light extract
2 1/2   pounds corn sugar
3   packages Vikera Hallertauer pellets (20 minutes)
3   teaspoons Irish moss
1   package Wine Art Burton salts
2   teaspoons Adolph's 100 percent natural meat
  tenderizer
10   pounds frozen raspberries (liquified)
3   packages Vierka lager yeast
1   teaspoon Kraus organic yeast nutrient
3   teaspoons gelatin finings
24   ounces corn sugar to prime

- Original specific gravity: 1.060
- Terminal specific gravity: 1.022
- Age when judged (since bottling): 7 1/2 months

Brewer's specifics
    Steep wort and raspberries for 30 minutes before diluting, cooling and pitching yeast. Rack after one week and add yeast nutrient and gelatin finings.

Judges' comments
    "Fantastic looking beer, Champagne-type bubbles. Aftertaste is slightly too tart, would like a bit more residual sweetness — excellent beer!"
    "The head fell rapidly. Very clean raspberry aroma leaps out at you. Raspberry flavor is perfect, one of the best I've tasted. This beer is a winner."
    "Crystal clear, lovely Champagne bubble appearance. Berry, berry nice raspberry nose and flavor."

Raspberry Dunkel Weizen

W.C. Embrey
Bellvue, Colorado
Third Place, Fruit Beer, 1988
(extract recipe)

Ingredients for 5 gallons
- 6 pounds William's weizen malt syrup
- 2 pounds dark dry malt extract
- 6 ounces chocolate malt
- 6 ounces dark crystal malt
- 6 ounces black patent malt
- 1 ounce Galena hops (60 minutes)
- 1 1/4 ounces Fuggles pellet hops (60 minutes)
- 1/2 ounce Cascade pellet hops (end of boil)
- 2 1/2 pounds frozen red raspberries
- 1 ounce maltodextrin (60 minutes)
- 1 packet Edme ale yeast
- 2/3 cup corn sugar

- Original specific gravity: not given
- Terminal specific gravity: not given
- Age when judged (since bottling): 3 months

Brewer's specifics
Grains are steeped in 120 degree F tap water for 5 minutes, then strained and sparged with tap water. Malt, maltodextrin and boiling hops are added and boiled 1 hour. Raspberries are mashed and added at end of boil.

Judges' comments
"The aroma is not unlike sweet corn initially, then it changes to a nutty, sherry-like, estery maltiness. Beautiful auburn color, with nice clarity and an adequate head. Nice flavor; elegantly robust, fruity, with a sherry-like quality. Big, intense, nearly liqueur-like ale. Complex and robust. Good effort!"
"Pleasant fruit aroma. Great clarity, color and head retention.

Fruit flavor comes through nicely; slightly subdued by hops, leaving a hops aftertaste."

Raspberry Royale
Ray Koenig
Greenfield, Wisconsin
Second Place, Specialty Beers, 1984
(extract recipe)

Ingredients for 5 gallons
    7 pounds Edme Superbrew light hop-flavored extract
    Edme lager yeast
    Raspberry extract

- Original specific gravity: 1.042
- Terminal specific gravity: 1.010
- Age when judged (since bottling): 4 1/2 months

Brewer's specifics
    Add 3/4 teaspoon raspberry extract per 144 ounces of beer at time of bottling.

Judges' comments
    "Nice malt/raspberry/hop balance. Wonderful raspberry; subtle and clear, delicate but not overwhelming. No off aroma. A real pleasure. Light body but good flavor. Exceptional. You ought to be real pleased with this one. A fine brew; no faults."
    "Specialty component is too withdrawn. Slight winey flavor — on the thin side perhaps."
    "Fruit character comes through pleasantly. Clean fermentation; somewhat bitter aftertaste for the fruity aroma."
    "Could use more head. Light aroma but pleasant. Bitter aftertaste could be lighter."

Raspberry Stout

Alphonse Conrad
Green Bay, Wisconsin
First Place, Specialty Beer, 1986
(extract recipe)

Ingredients for 6 gallons
- 3 1/3   pounds John Bull dark unhopped malt extract
- 3 1/3   pounds Edme SuperBrew light hopped malt extract
- 1 1/2   pounds crystal malt
- 1   pound chocolate malt
- 1   teaspoon gypsum
- 1   pound corn sugar
- 2   pounds dark dry malt extract
- 4 1/2   pounds fresh frozen raspberries
- 2   ounces Hallertauer hop pellets
- 2   packages Edme yeast
- 1   cup corn sugar to prime

- Original specific gravity: 1.060
- Terminal specific gravity: 1.020
- Age when judged (since bottling): 5 months

Brewer's specifics
Add crystal and chocolate malts to 1 1/2 gallons of water. When boiling starts, remove spent grains and add both cans of malt syrup, 1 pound of corn sugar, gypsum, and 1/3 of the hops. Bring to a boil. After 20 minutes, add another 1/3 of the hops. After another 20 minutes, add the last of the hops, add raspberries and turn off heat. Let steep for 15 minutes. Pour into open fermenter, let cool, pitch yeast and let ferment for 5 days.

After 5 days, boil 1 gallon of water with 2 pounds of dark dry malt and place into secondary fermenter, rack beer into secondary and let sit until gravity stabilizes, then bottle.

Judges' comments
"Too carbonated! All head! Very raspberry—downright intriguing flavor combination. Acidity covered nicely by raspberry. I bet it's dynamite a little younger."

"Nice deep burgundy color. Clear. Overcarbonated, but good head retention. Full berry aroma. Perfect blend of malt and berry flavors. Perfect dry aftertaste balances the initial raspberry flavor."

"Lovely dark ruby color. Overcarbonated! Great raspberry aroma — makes my mouth water. Since I'm partial to raspberries, I was excited about this stout and it didn't let me down. Good clean stout. I love it!"

Cherry Beer
Matthew Mueller
Baltimore, Maryland
Second Place, Specialty Beer, 1986
(all-grain recipe)

Ingredients for 5 gallons
- 7 pounds pale 6 row-malt
- 1 1/2 pounds Munich malt
- 1/2 pound wheat malt
- 10 pounds pitted sour cherries
- 1 teaspoon gypsum
- 1 teaspoon Irish moss
- 1 ounce Bullion hops (boil 60 minutes)
- 1/2 ounce Tettnanger hops (boil 60 minutes)
- 1/2 ounce Willamette hops (finish 3 minutes)
- 1 packet Edme ale yeast
- 3/4 cup corn sugar to prime

- Original specific gravity: 1.050
- Terminal specific gravity: 1.004
- Age when judged (since bottling): 10 1/2 months

Brewer's specifics
Mash all grains for 2 hours at 157 degrees F in 3 gallons of water with gypsum. Sparge with 6 gallons of water at 175 degrees F. Boil wort for 1 hour with Irish moss. Place macerated cherries with 2 gallons boiled wort and hold at 170 degrees F for 30 minutes. Cool wort, pitch yeast, and allow to ferment for 6 days. Skim floating

cherry debris. After 2 more days transfer to closed glass fermenter. Condition for one additional month. Rack and bottle.

Judges' comments
    "Could be clearer; good cherry color; good head retention (a little lace along the side of the glass). The cherry aroma comes through nicely (and delicately). A clean beer with just the right amount of cherry flavor. You've done a great favor for these cherries! I can find very little fault with this beer. Good job!"
    "Slight chill haze — cleared up as it warmed — nice reddish color, good head with small bubbles. Good balance. Can taste the hop bitterness with the cherry taste. The flavor is a cherry sourness with a sharp, tart aftertaste that does not detract from the beer. I would like to have one after dinner!"

Cherry Lager
Gary Bauer
Milwaukee, Wisconsin
First Place, All Grain Specialty Beers, 1984
(all-grain recipe)

Ingredients for 5 gallons
    6   pounds six-row barley malt
    1   pound Munich malt
    1/2 pound wheat malt
    2   pounds sour cherries
    2 1/4 ounces Saaz hops
    4   ounces liquid lager yeast
    3/4 cup priming sugar

- Original specific gravity: 1.050
- Terminal specific gravity: 1.016
- Approximate temperature of fermentation: 50 degrees F
- Age when judged (since bottling): 2 weeks

Brewer's specifics
    Mash grains at 158 degrees F for 1 1/2 hours. Sparge with water

at 170 degrees F to collect 6 gallons. Boil wort for a total of 1 1/2 hours. At 30 minutes add 1/2 ounce hops. At 45 minutes add another 1/2 ounce, and at 60 minutes another ounce.

Sparge and dry hop with 1/4 ounce Saaz hops. Cool to 60 degrees F and pitch yeast.

After one week, rack into another primary and add crushed cherries in a bag.

In another week remove cherries, rack to a carboy and condition two weeks in an air-locked fermenter. Bottle when fermentation is complete.

Judges' comments

"Overpriming caused yeast sweeping. Estery — could have more hops. Slight pit flavor is not unpleasant. George Washington would be proud of you. I want to make this beer!"

"Cherry and beer flavors come through. After harshness but a good front or mouth cherry flavor. Would have scored higher if harshness could be corrected."

"Clarity needs improvement. Very, very good bouquet. Outstanding overall flavor, great blending of flavors."

Red Ryder

Pat O'Hara
Bedford, Ohio
First Place, Fruit Beer, 1988
(all-grain recipe)

Ingredients for 7 gallons
- 5 pounds Briess 6-row pale malted barley
- 3 pounds Munton & Fison malted wheat
- 1 pound Munich malt
- 1 pound cara-pils malt
- 1 ounce Hallertauer leaf hops (60 minutes)
- 1 ounce Hallertauer leaf hops (1 minute, then steep for 1 hour)
- 6 pounds red raspberries

> 2 teaspoons pectic enzyme
> 1 package Red Star lager yeast
> 1 cup dextrose to prime

- Original specific gravity: 1.080
- Terminal specific gravity: 1.020
- Age when judged (since bottling): 9 months

Brewer's specifics

Add raspberries and pectic enzyme to one gallon of hot water and steep for three hours. Strain and add to cool wort.

Judges' comments

"Aroma is there and the color and clarity are nicely done, but it lacks carbonation. Raspberry flavor is great, lacks body slightly. Very good."

"Berry, berry, raspberry, just like sniffing a box of fruit. Very difficult to detect any hops or malt. Looks like a mead. Kinda reddish orange, little to no head, tiny bubbles, clear. A lot of the sourness of the raspberries was retained as well as some of the astringency, light body, winey. Remember to keep in mind that beers are to be balanced. I would cut back on the amount of raspberries, leaving everything else the same and you'll have an awesome beer."

HERB BEER

Herb Beer. Any ale or lager using herbs or spices other than hops to create distinct qualities.

Dopple-Bark
Jim Lister
Coralville, Iowa
Second Place, Herb Beer, 1987
(extract recipe)

Ingredients for 5 gallons
         8   pounds Alexander malt extract syrup
         1   pound crystal malt
         1   quart maple syrup
       1/2   ounce spruce essence
       1/2   ounce maple extract
         1   teaspoon Irish moss
     2 1/4   ounces Cluster hops (60 minutes)
       1/2   ounce Cascade hops (20 minutes)
         1   package Wyeast liquid ale yeast
       7/8   cup dextrose to prime

• Original specific gravity: 1.075
• Terminal specific gravity: not available
• Age when judged (since bottling): 1 month

Brewer's specifics
    Steep crystal malt 30 minutes. Add maple syrup with malt
extract. Add spruce essence and maple extract with Irish moss last
10 minutes.

Filmore Christmas Ale 87
Mike Sternick
Denver, Colorado
Third Place, Herb Beer, 1988
(extract recipe)

Ingredients for 5 gallons
         7   pounds Munton & Fison light dry malt extract
       1/2   pound crystal malt
       1/8   pound black patent malt
         1   pound clover honey

2 ounces Cascade hops (60 minutes)
1 ounce Hallertauer hops (2 minutes)
1 ounce Cascade hops (2 minutes)
1 ounce ginger root (12 minutes)
6 inch stick of cinnamon (12 minutes)
4 teaspoons orange peel (12 minutes)
1 package Edme yeast
3/4 cup dextrose to prime

Brewer's specifics
• Original specific gravity: 1.050 - 1.054
• Terminal specific gravity: 1.019 - 1.025
• Age when judged (since bottling): 9 months

Judges' comments
"Orange and ginger evident in aroma. Looks clean and clear. Dryness from honey and cinnamon combine for a pleasant aftertaste. I like the progression of aroma and flavors from all spices."

"Very complex nose. Ginger distinct but muted/masked by fragrant spicy sweet (presumably orange and cinnamon). Appearance absolutely gorgeous. Like a continental dark (though on the light side). Very nicely balanced, tastes well-aged, orange, cinnamon and ginger all come through, but none dominate. Excellent beer, though I would have preferred more alcohol."

Hi-Res Root Beer

Wayne Waananen
Denver, Colorado
First Place, Herb Beer, 1987
(extract recipe)

Ingredients for 5 gallons
3 pounds Munton & Fison amber dry malt extract
2 1/5 pounds Premier hopped malt extract syrup
1/2 pound crystal malt
1/4 pound chocolate malt
1 1/2 teaspoons Zatarain's root beer extract
1 teaspoon Irish moss (30 minutes)

      1   ounce Cascade leaf hops (60 minutes)
    1/2   ounce Cascade leaf hops (10 minutes)
    1/2   ounce Cascade leaf hops (after boil)
      2   packages Muntona yeast
    2/3   cup dextrose to prime

- Original specific gravity: 1.045
- Terminal specific gravity: 1.018
- Age when judged (since bottling): 2 months

Brewer's specifics

Added 1 1/4 teaspoon root beer extract last 10 minutes of boil. After 10 minutes removed from heat, added last of hops and force-cooled with wort chiller. After reaching 90 degrees F (about 15 minutes) sparged into carboy and pitched yeast. Racked into secondary at seven days. At kegging added 1/4 teaspoon root beer extract along with dextrose.

Judges' comments

"Aroma is really malty, rootbeery, inviting. Appearance is really great — couldn't be better! Fruit beery rooty tooty. This is a must on a hot, dry, dusty day. You have made a great effort."

"Wow! Yep, root beer. Nice aroma. I get a hint of hops too. Very nice appearance, with a nice creamy head. The flavor is a bit heavy on black patent malt. A cleanly brewed beer. I suggest less bitterness, which would improve the balance (in my mind)."

"Root beer aroma comes through. Nice creamy head despite the large bubbles. Root beer flavor comes through very nicely. Hearty and robust aroma, taste and aftertaste. An admirable attempt for the category. Good work."

Rag Time Black Ale

Tim Mead
Boulder, Colorado
First Place, Herb Beers, 1979
(extract recipe)

Ingredients for 13 gallons
      2   gallons water

    6 pounds dark dried malt
6 1/2 pounds John Bull dark malt
    4 ounces hops (plus one ounce Cascade hops optional)
  1/4 teaspoon Irish moss
    5 teaspoons gypsum
    2 teaspoons salt
    1 pound black patent malt
    2 pounds crystal malt
  1/2 ounce cinnamon bark
    5 pounds sugar
       ale yeast

Brewer's specifics
   All the grains were mashed for 1 hour. The rest of the ingredients were added and boiled for an additional hour. Finally, steep the cinnamon bark in wort. Then add 5 pounds sugar to primary fermenter.
   Ale yeast was added at 74 degrees F for a resulting hydrometer reading of 1.048.

Ring-tailed Lemur Lager

Pamela Moore and Kurt Denke
Philadelphia, Pennsylvania
First Place, Herb Beer, 1988
(extract recipe)

Ingredients for 5 gallons
3 1/3 pounds John Bull light hopped malt extract syrup
    3 pounds clover honey
    3 ounces diced ginger root
    3 ounces Budweiser baking yeast
  3/4 cup dextrose to prime

- Original specific gravity: 1.040
- Terminal specific gravity: 1.004
- Age when judged (since bottling): 2 1/2 months

Judges' comments
    "Delicate ginger aroma. Clean, clear, golden light lager. Ginger comes through up front and aftertaste. Distinct honey taste there, but surprisingly weak (not much used?). Very nice, drinkable, thirst-quenching beer."
    "Nice ginger aroma that lingers. Clean and clear. Ginger and honey evident. Honey fermentation gives a nice, dry taste. Very nice effort. Pleasant drink. Nothing overpowers another ingredient."

Herb Beer

Jodi Smith
Loveland, Colorado
Second Place, Specialty Beers, 1984
(all-grain recipe)

Ingredients for 4 gallons
        6 pounds pale malt
    1/2 ounce Bullion hops (45 minutes)
        1 ounce fresh yarrow leaf (45 minutes)
    1/2 ounce Bullion hops (30 minutes)
        1 ounce fresh yarrow leaf (30 minutes)
            Edme ale yeast

- Original specific gravity: 1.038
- Terminal specific gravity: 1.004
- Age when judged (since bottling): 30 days

Brewer's specifics
    Mash grain for 1 1/4 hours at 125 degrees F, 3/4 hour at 140 degrees F, 1/2 hour at 150 degrees F. Sparge by stretching cheesecloth over a large pot, spread mash on cloth and pour boiling water through it. Keep in secondary for 18 weeks.

Judges' comments
    "The yarrow is overly prevalent — it masks out any other flavors that may contribute to a greater complexity of the beer."

"A unique flavor that comes through clearly and strongly."

"A slight yeast sweeping after opened (appearance). Aroma is yarrow — yarrow — yarrow. Slight acid aftertaste. What a great combo — not the usual but a new pleasure."

OZ

Ray Spangler
Erlanger, Kentucky
Second Place, Herb Beer, 1988
(all-grain recipe)

Ingredients for 13 gallons

18	pounds mild ale malted barley
3	pounds Munich malt (toasted 200 degrees F for 3 hours)
2	pounds wheat malt
1 1/2	pounds crystal malt
2	ounces Hallertauer hops (60 minutes)
2	ounces Tettnanger hops (60 minutes)
1	ounce Northern Brewer hops (30 minutes)
2	ounces Hallertauer hops (30 minutes)
1	ounce Tettnanger hops (30 minutes)
1	ounce Cascade hops (after boil)
1	ounce Tettnanger hops (after boil)
39	grams gypsum
1/2	ounce coriander (60 minutes)
1/2	ounce coriander (end of boil)
1	ounce coriander (dry hopped)
	home cultured Chimay Red Yeast
4	ounces dextrose and 4 ounces dry malt extract to prime

- Original specific gravity: 1.025
- Terminal specific gravity: 1.005
- Age when judged (since bottling): 2 months

Brewer's specifics

"This was 6 gallons of second runnings from a split batch.

Infusion/decoction mash used; strike temperature 156 degrees F for one hour. Decoction of 6 gallons mash boiled for 10 minutes. Temperature raise to 166 degrees F for 45 minutes. Mash ended.

Judges' comments
"Great sweet, clean aroma. Buttery bouquet, very nice. Great color, perhaps a bit more carbonation is needed. Add more sugar during the priming stage. Nice unique flavor. A bit bitter, but a nice bitter. Leaves a slight aftertaste (probably from coriander). Nice balance. Great unique taste. Perhaps cut down a wee bit on the coriander. Very drinkable."

"Hops and coriander evident in aroma. Looks to be clean and clear. The hops and coriander bitterness linger No ingredient overpowering. Very nice beer, well-balanced. A pleasant drink!"

Vampire Ale

Ron Page
Middletown, Connecticut
First Place, Specialty Beer, 1988
(all-grain recipe)

Ingredients for 25 gallons

55	pounds ale malt
16 1/2	pounds Laaglander light dry malt extract
2	pounds Vienna malt
1	pound Cara-pils malt
5	ounces Cascade hops (boil)
2 1/2	ounces Hallertauer hops (boil)
2 1/2	ounces Tettnanger hops (boil)
2 1/2	ounces Hallertauer hops (finish)
2 1/2	ounces Tettnanger hops (finish)
15	pounds honey
1 3/4	ounces beechwood chips
8 3/4	ounces lactose
1 1/4	ounces orange rind
5	packages Edme yeast

- Original specific gravity: 1.080
- Terminal specific gravity: 1.023
- Age when judged (since bottling): unknown

Brewer's specifics
　　All grains mashed at 152 to 155 degrees F for 1 hour.

Judges' comments
　　"Elegant bouquet, wonderful! Beautiful appearance! Subtle expression of honey. All flavors were well represented. Very well balanced. Excellent use of these ingredients with a resulting brew that's very satisfying."
　　"Very pleasing, good balance of hops to malt with elegant orange aroma. Beautiful appearance! You could read a book through it, it sparkles. The flavor comes on. Makes you want to drink more. Outstanding for style."

PALE ALE

Pale Ale. In England, an amber- or copper-colored, top-fermented beer brewed with very hard water and pale malts. It is the bottled equivalent of bitter, but drier, hoppier and lighter. The adjective pale in this instance distinguishes it from darker brews such as brown ale, stout and porter. Pale ales are brewed from original wort gravities of 1.043 to 1.053 (11 to 14 degrees Balling) and contain about 3.4 percent alcohol by volume. Classics of this style include Bass Pale and Worthington's White Shield.

Pale ales are sometimes called Burton ales because this style of beer originated from the popular versions brewed in Burton-on-Trent in the 1780s.

British Bitter. In Britain, bitter is the draft equivalent of pale ale. It is a golden-brown or copper-colored top-fermented beer usually highly hopped, dry and lightly carbonated. It accounts for about 80 percent of draft beer sales in English pubs.

Bitter is slightly more alcoholic (3.0 to 5.5 percent by volume) and more heavily hopped than mild (with which it is sometimes mixed). It is usually available in three strengths although there are regional variations: ordinary bitter, OG 1.035 to 1.040 (9 to 10 degrees Balling); best bitter, OG 1.040 to 1.048 (10 to 12 degrees Balling); and special or strong bitter, OG 1.055 to 1.065 (14 to 16 degrees Balling).

Traditionally, bitter is unpasteurized and cask-conditioned in the pub cellar. In the 1960s the large brewing companies introduced kegged-beer, a filtered, pasteurized, chilled and artificially carbonated bitter. A consumer campaign initiated by CAMRA (Campaign for Real Ale) in the 1970s opposed this new trend. As a result naturally conditioned casked bitter is again available as Real Ale.

India Pale Ale. This style of beer was brewed in England for British troops stationed in India in the 18th century. It was brewed very strong to survive a voyage that could take as long as six months. The term now refers to bottled pale ales, especially those intended for exportation.

IPAs have a healthy alcoholic content (5.0 percent by volume) and a high hopping rate. The bouquet of this copper-colored classic is a full-flowery hop experience. The use of water high in mineral salts in conjunction with the hops creates a dry brew with an assertive hop bitterness.

Boulder Light Ale

Stephen Carpenter
Boulder, Colorado
First Place, Pale Ale, 1983
(extract recipe)

Ingredients for 6 1/2 gallons
3 1/2 pounds Edme DMS malt extract
3 1/3 pounds John Bull light extract
1/4 pound crystal malt (crushed)
1 teaspoon Burton water salts
2 ounces Saaz hop pellets
1/4 teaspoon Irish moss
1/4 pound brown sugar
1/2 ounce Hallertauer pellets
1 package Edme ale yeast
1 package Arayer yeast
1 1/3 cups priming sugar

- Original specific gravity: 1.042
- Terminal specific gravity: 1.013
- Approximate temperature of fermentation: 60 degrees F
- Age when judged (since bottling): 3 1/2 weeks

Brewer's specifics
Heat in 2 quarts of water at 120 degrees F for 1 hour: the crystal malt, extracts and Burton water salts. Sparge and boil for 1 hour with the Saaz pellets. Add Irish moss for the last 15 minutes of the boil. Add brown sugar for the last 5 minutes of the boil. Add Hallertauer pellets for the last minute of the boil. Add water to make 6 1/2 gallons and pitch yeast at 70 to 78 degrees F. After one week in primary, rack to secondary and continue fermentation for 3 weeks or until complete. Bottle with priming sugar.

Judges' comments
"Very good light ale; excellent balance and flavor."
"A good drinkable ale; a little low on carbonation. Excellent."
"Excellent ale. A bit more carbonation needed."
"Fine brew. Lacking a bit of carbonation. Love the bouquet."

Light-Bodied Light Ale

Stephen Carpenter
Boulder, Colorado
First Place, Pale Ale, 1982
(extract recipe)

Ingredients for 8 gallons
6 1/2   pounds John Bull plain light malt extract
2 1/2   pounds Munton & Fison dry amber malt extract
1/2   pound crystal malt
2   ounces Cascade hops
1/2   pound dark brown sugar
2   teaspoons Burton water treatment salts
1/2   ounce Hallertauer hops
1 1/3   cups corn sugar for bottling
       Edme ale yeast

• Original specific gravity: 1.044

Brewer's specifics
   Boil for 1 hour: 2 gallons of water, malts, Cascade hops, brown sugar and water salts. Add Hallertauer hops during final 5 minutes of boil. Sparge hot wort into primary and add cold water to make 8 gallons. Add yeast when temperature is below 80 degrees F. Rack into secondary fermenter on second or third day. Ferment in secondary until complete, then bottle with 1 1/3 cups sugar.

Sandy's Ale

Stephen Carpenter
Boulder, Colorado
First Place, Pale Ale, 1981
(extract recipe)

Ingredients for 6 1/2 gallons
3 1/2   pounds Edme DMS malt extract
3 3/4   pounds Munton & Fison dry amber malt extract

    2   ounces Cascade leaf hop
  1/2   ounce Hallertauer hop pellets
    2   teaspoons Burton water treatment salts
  1/4   teaspoon Irish moss
1 1/2   pounds corn sugar (plus 1 1/4 cups for bottling)
        ale yeast
  1/4   teaspoon ascorbic acid

- Original specific gravity: 1.046
- Terminal specific gravity: 1.010

Brewer's specifics

Boil the malt extracts, Cascade hops and Burton salts in two gallons of water for about two hours. Add the Hallertauer hops and Irish moss for the last 10 minutes of boiling. Dissolve the corn sugar in the hot wort and sparge into the primary fermenter. Add the Hallertauer hops and enough water to bring volume to 6 1/2 gallons. Cool to 80 degrees and add ale yeast.

After primary fermentation is complete, the brew should be racked into a secondary fermenter and held for about one month. Bottling was done after adding the ascorbic acid and priming sugar at a final specific gravity of 1.010.

Fraternity House Ale

Ron Page
Middletown, Connecticut
First Place, Pale Ale, 1988
(all-grain recipe)

Ingredients for 25 gallons
     30   pounds pale ale malt
  5 1/2   pounds crystal malt
  1 1/2   pounds cara-pils malt
    1/2   pound Munich malt
 12 3/4   ounces Cascade hops (boil)
 10 1/2   ounces Willamette hops (boil)

5 1/4 ounces Cascade hops (finish)
1 3/4 ounces Kent Goldings hops (dry hopped)
1 3/4 ounces Willamette hops (dry hopped)
5 1/4 ounces Cascade hops (dry hopped)
        Muntona yeast
     6 pounds honey to prime

- Original specific gravity: 1.070
- Terminal specific gravity: 1.024
- Age when judged (since bottling): unknown

Brewer's specifics
Mash all grains at 150 to 155 degrees F for 1 1/2 hours.

Judges' comments
"O boy! Beautiful spicy hoppy aroma with lots of malt in background. Good clarity. Amber red tint. Good malt-hop balance although sweetness overpowers slightly."

"Very balanced, nice hop nose with malt background. Great Cascade. Very nice, clean appearance. Nice malty flavor with great hop balance. Nice dry hop finish, rich. Very delicious beer, you've got a winner here! Great IPA!"

No. 7

Phillip Moeller
Sacramento, California
First Place, Pale Ale, 1985
(all-grain recipe)

Ingredients for 5 gallons
     8 pounds pale malted barley
   1/2 pound crystal malt
   3/4 ounce Bullion hop pellets (95 minutes)
   3/4 ounce Galena hop pellets (95 minutes)
   3/4 ounce Galena hops (1 hour)
   3/4 ounce Cascade leaf hops (1 hour)
     1 teaspoon citric acid (1/2 in mash, 1/2 in sparge)
     1 teaspoon gypsum

1/4 teaspoon MgSO$_4$ (Epsom salts)
2 packets Muntona ale yeast
1 cup corn sugar to prime

- Original specific gravity: 1.050
- Terminal specific gravity: 1.019
- Single-stage fermentation in glass for 4 days at 65 degrees F, 8 days at 35 degrees F
- Age when judged (since bottling): 7 weeks

Brewer's specifics
Modified decoction mash. Add grain to 13 quarts water at 140 degrees F; stabilize at 128 for 10 minutes. Remove two quarts, heat to boiling and retuurn to mash; stabilize at 132 for 10 minutes. Remove one quart, heat to boil and return to mash; stabilize at 136 for 20 minutes. Remove 3 1/2 quarts, heat to boil and return to mash; stabilize at 152 for one hour. Sparge with 19 1/2 quarts water at 167 degrees F for one hour.

Judges' comments
"Excellent clarity, head, color and bead; small bubbles. Nice winey front hop nose, malty follow up; very good. Smooth body, good balance, good hop aftertaste. Excellent brew!"
"Great job! Hop aroma comes through, though there's a bit of harshness or apple note in aroma. Very smooth flavor. Strawberry ester comes through with taste, nice and subtle. Use of fresh hops evident. Well balanced."

Pale Mountain Ale

Randy Lieb
Santa Rosa, California
First Place, Pale Ale, 1987
(all-grain recipe)

Ingredients for 5 gallons
11 pounds pale ale malt
1 pound crystal malt

     1   teaspoon gypsum
  1/2   teaspoon magnesium suflate (Epsom salts)
  1/2   ounce Galena hops (40 minutes)
  1/2   ounce Galena hops (20 minutes)
  1/4   ounce Galena hops (15 minutes)
     1   package Red Star ale yeast
     1   cup light dry malt extract to prime

- Original specific gravity: 1.040
- Terminal specific gravity: 1.010
- Age when judged (since bottling): 10 months

Brewer's specifics

    (Protein rest) mash 45 minutes at 124 degrees F. Starch conversion: 45 minutes at 158 degrees F. Sparge 20 minutes at 170 degrees F.

Bitter

Peter Goss
Swansea, Massachusetts
Second Place, Pale Ale, 1983
(extract recipe)

Ingredients for 5 gallons
3 4/5   pounds Munton & Fison amber hopped extract
    1   pound Munton & Fison light dry extract
    2   cups crystal malt, crushed
    3   cups corn sugar
    1   cup dark brown sugar
    1   ounce Brewers Gold hop pellets
    1   ounce Cascade hop pellets
    2   teaspoons gypsum
    1   teaspoon Irish moss
    1   cup priming sugar

- Original specific gravity: 1.038

- Terminal specific gravity: 1.008
- Approximate temperature of fermentation: 65 degrees F

Brewer's specifics

Mash the crystal malt in 5 quarts water at 150 degrees F for 1 hour. Sparge with 1 quart hot water. Add malt extracts, corn sugar, brown sugar, gypsum and boil for 30 minutes. Add Irish moss and 1/2 ounce Brewers Gold pellets and boil 15 minutes more. Add other 1/2 ounce of Brewers Gold pellets and continue to boil for 10 minutes. Add the Cascade pellets and strain to primary. Add water to make 5 gallons and pitch yeast at 70 to 78 degrees F.

Rack to secondary after 1 week and continue fermentation for 2 weeks. Bottle with priming sugar.

Judges' comments

"Good all around light ale, very acceptable."

"A good drinkable ale."

"Seemed to lose carbonation a bit quickly, but overall a good ale."

"Very fine bouquet (almost fruity); excellent balance in the taste and an enjoyable aftertaste. Just a great all around beer."

Great Baddow Bitter

Gary Brown
West St. Paul, Minnesota
Second Place, Pale Ale, 1987
(extract recipe)

Ingredients for 5 gallons

     6 2/3 pounds John Bull light malt extract syrup
       1/2 pound crystal malt
         3 ounces black patent malt
         1 ounce Northern Brewer hops (60 minutes)
   1 1/2 ounces Cascade hops (30 minutes)
         1 ounce Fuggles hops (30 minutes' steep after boil)
         1 teaspoon gypsum

    1   teaspoon Irish moss (15 minutes)
    2   packages Edme ale yeast
    1/2 cup dextrose to prime

* Original specific gravity: 1.042
* Terminal specific gravity: 1.020
* Age when judged (since bottling): 2 months

Judges' comments
    "Alcohol and maltiness overwhelm the nose, though the hops
are perceptible; a superb crystal clear beer, a bit dark for a bitter
though not out of the category. Malt/hop balance is pretty good
but alcohol overbalances this beer. Very nice overall; a little dry on
the finish."
    "Gentle but nose-worrying bouquet. Deep, nice color. Clear.
Pinpoint bubbles. Nice Belgian lace. The taste is more simple than
I expected from the look and scent. Very clean but too simple. Not
enough intrigue."

Crawford and Scriven Best Bitter

Dennis Crawford and Richard Scriven
Casper, Wyoming
First Place, British Bitter, 1985
(all-grain recipe)

Ingredients for 5 gallons
    9   pounds pale malt
    8   ounces crystal malt
    3   ounces Munich malt
    2   ounces chocolate malt
    1   teaspoon gypsum (in mash)
    1   teaspoon gypsum (in boil)
    1   ounce Galena leaf hops (90 minutes)

1 ounce Cascade pellet hops (90 minutes)
1/2 ounce Hersbrucker leaf hops (30 minutes)
1 ounce Hersbrucker leaf hops (3 minutes)
Danish ale yeast
1 cup corn sugar to prime

- Original specific gravity: 1.043
- Terminal specific gravity: 1.009
- Single-stage fermentation in glass at 60 degrees F for one week
- Age when judged (since bottling): 3 1/2 months

Brewer's specifics

Mash at 92 degrees F for 45 minutes; 128 for 1 1/2 hours; 135 for 15 minutes; 156 for one hour. Bring to 167 degrees and sparge with water at 165.

Judges' comments

"Very clear, faintly pink tones in color; good bead. Lightly fruity and hoppy nose. Lightly fruity flavor with some perfumey hop taste; salty finish."

"Nice clarity and carbonation is appropriate to the class. Light hoppy aroma; slightly salty taste. Excellent effort; a very drinkable beer."

I Couldn't Decide

Nancy Vineyard
Santa Rosa, California
First Place, British Bitter, 1984
(all-grain recipe)

Ingredients for 5 gallons

8 pounds pale malt (Briess precracked)
1 pound wheat malt
1/2 pound Munich malt
1/2 pound crystal malt

3/4   ounce Northern Brewer hops
1/4   ounce Spalt hops
1/4   ounce Styrian Golding hops
3/4   ounce Saaz hops
1/2   ounce Hallertauer hops
  1   teaspoon gypsum
  1   teaspoon salt
  2   packages Muntona ale yeast
3/4   cup priming sugar

- Original specific gravity: 1.040
- Terminal specific gravity: 1.012
- Approximate temperature of fermentation: 58 - 60 degrees F.
- Age when judged (since bottling): 23 days

Brewer's specifics

Three-step infusion mash: Mash the grains in 3 gallons of water. After 20 minutes raise the temperature from 95 degrees F to 126; hold for 20 minutes. After 10 minutes raise to 136 degrees F and hold for 20 minutes. After 20 minutes raise to 156 degrees F and hold for 10 minutes.

Sparge with 4 1/2 gallons water at 170 degrees F.

For one hour boil mashing liquor, gypsum, salt, 1/2 ounce Northern Brewer hops and Spalt hops. For the last 30 minutes of that boil add Styrian Golding, 1/2 ounce Saaz and 1/4 ounce Northern Brewer hops. Finish with Hallertauer and 1/2 ounce Saaz hops when wort is at 150 degrees F.

Sparge into primary. Let cool to 60 degrees and pitch yeast.

In 5 days rack into secondary and keep there for 8 hours. Bottle with priming sugar.

Judges' comments

"Good color, but lack of clarity lets this down. Interesting hop/malt balance with a clean nose."

"Good head quality. Bready aroma with underlying maltiness. Excellent balance. Harsh in finish. Husky/grainy flavor with phenolic overtones, possible oversparging or too hot sparge water."

"Slightly cloudy, good color, fair head retention. Nice combination of grain and hops in the nose. The flavor has a good character of IPA style bitter, not heavy enough on the malt though. Good beer."

Stumptown Ale

Jeff Frane
Portland, Oregon
First Place, British Bitter, 1986
(all-grain recipe)

Ingredients for 5 gallons
    10 pounds Klages malt
    1/2 pound crystal malt
    1/4 pound flaked maize
    1 ounce Fuggles hop pellets (boil 75 minutes)
    1 1/2 ounces Fuggles hop pellets (boil 60 minutes)
    1/2 ounce Fuggles hop pellets (end of boil)
    2 teaspoons gypsum
        home cultured ale yeast
    1/2 cup corn sugar to prime

- Original specific gravity: 1.054
- Terminal specific gravity: 1.016
- Age when judged (since bottling): 4 months

Brewer's specifics
    Mash with 4 gallons water. Mash in at 116 degrees F; raise to 122 degrees F in 30 minutes; hold 30 minutes; raise to 140 degrees F in 20 minutes; hold 10 minutes; raise to 154 degrees F; hold 30 minutes; raise to 176 degrees F; sparge with 5 gallons 165-degree F water.

Judges' comments
    "Good overall appearance—nice head retention. Pleasant aroma—well balanced, slight ester present. Very good flavor—assertive hops and a hint of malt sweetness. Could use a little more body."

"Dense head. Delicate color, but well within limits of style. Hoppy aroma. Hop accented. Some sweetness. A pleasant beer, with an enjoyable hoppiness, especially in the aroma."

Groids India Pale Ale

Mark Glasset
Salt Lake City, Utah
First Place, Pale Ale, 1985
(extract recipe)

Ingredients for 5 gallons
- 7 pounds Munton and Fison light dry malt extract
- 1 pound crystal malt
- 1/2 pound pale malt
- 2 ounces Brewers Gold hops (45 minutes)
- 1 ounce Cascade hops (hot wort poured through them in strainer at sparge)
- 2 teaspoons gypsum
- 2 packets Edme ale yeast
- 3/4 cup corn sugar to prime

- Age when judged (since bottling): 4 months

Brewer's specifics
Toast the pale malt in the oven at 350 degrees F for 10 minutes. "Extra cleanliness seems to have paid off on this one. New procedures included steaming of the hops 5 minutes prior to use, omitting the use of a hydrometer, not stirring the yeast into the wort and single-stage fermentation in glass as usual. I have to give credit where it's due — this is a modified Papazian recipe."

Judges' comments
"Color is a bit dark, but rich; head is a little thin. Hoppy and rich aroma. The flavor is strong on hops and grainy; nice fruitiness, full and hearty."

"Check your carbonation, it's somewhat flat. Nice malt nose; good full-bodied flavor, nice hop aftertaste."

"Has a slight fruity flavor, yet a well balanced tasty ale!"

"Good color, clarity and head. Only fair head retention. Nice dry hop nose, not floral. Fair body. A good drinking beer. No flaws but few high points."

India Pale Ale
Jay Conner
San Rafael, California
Seond Place, Pale Ale, 1981
(extract recipe)

This ale was an attempt to duplicate India Pale Ale, which is oak aged, and made with Brewer's Gold hops. Instead of a barrel, Jay used oak chips, and lacking true Brewer's Gold, he used a sister strain of hops called Bullion.

Ingredients for 5 gallons
- 3 pounds Great Fermentations bulk light malt
- 3 pounds British light dry malt extract
- 6 tablespoons Bullion hop pellets
- 2 teaspoons gypsum
- 1 teaspoon salt
   handful of oak chips
   Kitzinger ale yeast
- 1 1/4 cups corn sugar (for bottling)

Brewer's specifics
Bring to a boil: the malt extract, two gallons of water, gypsum, salt and two tablespoons of hop pellets. After 30 minutes of boiling add another tablespoon of hop pellets. After 15 more minutes add another tablespoon of hop pellets. After five more minutes turn off the heat.

Add the remaining two tablespoons of hops and oak chips to the primary fermenter and pour the hot wort over them. Fill the primary fermenter with additional hot water to bring the volume to five gallons and allow to cool over night while covered.

Pitch a yeast starter of ale yeast the following morning.

Do not skim head during primary fermentation. Rack the brew and use a glass secondary fermenter. Allow to ferment in secondary fermenter for four weeks.

When bottling, prime with corn sugar.

Jay notes: "Next time I'll use more oak, more aromatic hops and less sugar."

XXX-IPA

Ray Spangler
Erlanger, Kentucky
First Place, India Pale Ale, 1986
(all-grain recipe)

Ingredients for 5 gallons

- 6 pounds pale malt
- 1 pound Munich malt
- 1 pound malted barley (6-row toasted 30 minutes at 350 degrees F)
- 1/2 pound wheat
- 3/4 pound crystal malt
- 2 teaspoons gypsum
- 1 ounce Brewers Gold and 1/2 ounce Bullion (60 minutes)
- 1 ounce Willamette (45 minutes)
- 1/2 ounce Willamette and 1/2 ounce Cascade (5 minutes)
- 15 grams Hallertau (dry hopped in secondary)
- 1/4 pound oak wood shavings added to secondary
  Edme ale yeast
- 3 1/2 ounces corn sugar and 1 1/2 ounces light dry malt extract boiled with a small amount of wort to prime

Brewer's specifics

Step mash procedures were used.

- Original specific gravity: 1.061
- Terminal specific gravity: 1.000
- Age when judged (since bottling): 8 months

Judges' comments

"Active head, but nice lacy bubbles, color a bit pale but OK. Mild hops, no malt. Good balance, strength kept under wraps, nice hops, needs malt sweetness to counterbalance hops and avoid thin taste."

"Great color and head. Good fresh hops and malt. Initial taste is better than finish. Slighly bitter finish that isn't from hops. Great overall beer. Perhaps a cleanliness problem hurts the final taste."

"Lovely and lively appearance. Aroma is sweet, hoppy, subdued. Flavor has good definition and OK aftertaste. Tastes like a slightly flavored mellow Anchor Steam. Don't boil/mash quite so long is my hunch. Also, perhaps needs a touch more crystal malt."

PORTER

Porter. A very bitter, very dark, almost black and mildly alcoholic top-fermented beer first brewed by a man named Harwood in Shoreditch, London, in 1730. Porter was a substitute for a then popular mix of ale, beer and twopenny called three-heads. It was called Entire and was advertised as being richer and more nourishing than ale. It was intended for porters, carters and other heavy laborers who would find in it the strength to accomplish tasks that no spirit drinker could perform. It was nicknamed porter's ale and, eventually, simply porter. Its dark color was derived from roasted, unmalted barley and sometimes

from a dash of licorice. A high hopping rate effectively lightens the mouth and gives a clean, quick finish to what otherwise would come through as a heavier beer.

In the British Isles, porter was overtaken in popularity by bitter stout during the 19th century, and the last British porter was brewed in Dublin in 1973. Porter is still brewed today, mostly by bottom fermentation, in East Germany, North and South America, Africa, China, Denmark, Hungary, Poland and Russia. London-style porter ranges in alcohol content between 5.0 and 7.5 percent by volume and varies in style from bitter to mild and sweet.

Eclipse

John W. and Nancy Ostrom
Davis, California
First Place, Porter, 1987
(extract recipe)

Ingredients for 6 gallons
- 6 pounds English dark bulk malt extract
- 2 pounds domestic light bulk malt extract
- 1 pound roasted barley
- 1 teaspoon Irish moss (30 minutes)
- 1/2 teaspoon citric acid
- 1 ounce Galena pellet hops (60 minutes)
- 1 1/2 ounces Northern Brewer pellet hops (30 minutes)
- 1 1/4 ounces Northern Brewer pellet hops (15 minutes)
- 3/4 ounce British blend pellet hops (5 minutes)
- 2 packages Muntona ale yeast
- 3/4 cups dextrose to prime

- Original specific gravity: not available
- Terminal specific gravity: not available
- Age when judged (since bottling): 9 1/2 months

Judges' comments
"Great hop and black malt aroma. Not opaque, excellent red hue comes through. The head is not too dark either, which happens

too often. Yep! This is a porter. Very good job. Body not too full."

"Nice hoppy aroma. Glass carefully poured was 2/3 head. Nice deep ruby red. Needs to be a bit darker. Real nice balance. Good medium body. Fairly even. Maybe a bit more intensity would be better for porters. Be bold. Nice job. Boost everything. Quite nice and very appropriate to style."

Essential Porter

Nancy Vineyard
Santa Rosa, California
First Place, Porter, 1986
(extract recipe)

Ingredients for 5 gallons

5	pounds Great Fermentations dry dark malt extract
2	pounds crystal malt
1 1/2	pounds Munich malt
1/4	pound black patent malt
1/2	pound wheat malt
4	ounces dextrin (100 percent)
1 1/2	ounces Nugget pellets
2	ounces Hallertauer hops (190 degrees F to cool, 1 hour)
2	packets Edme ale yeast
1/2	cup corn sugar to prime

- Original specific gravity: 1.052
- Terminal specific gravity: 1.012
- Age when judged (since bottling): 7 1/2 months

Brewer's specifics

Mashed all grains 150 degrees F for 30 minutes. Boil 3/4 ounce Nugget pellets for 30 minutes, then add the other 3/4 ounce and boil for 30 minutes.

Judges' comments

"Good clarity! Complex aroma — spicy. Flavor doesn't keep up with aroma. Needs more malt. Some roastiness would help."

"Very nice color. Clean nose, all finishing hops. Nice bitter flavor, not heavy but evident. Problem-free."

"Clean, clear and creamy. Nice finishing hop. Beautiful hop nose. Light malt. Lighter bitter than most porters. Well balanced."

Fetch, Porter

Ted Badgerow
Ann Arbor, Michigan
Second place, Porter, 1987
(extract recipe)

Ingredients for 5 gallons

- 6 2/3   pounds BierKeller Dark malt extract syrup
- 4   pounds Munton and Fison dark dry malt extract
- 1   ounce Saaz hop pellets (boil)
- 2   ounces Hallertauer whole hops (boil)
- 1   ounce Tettnanger hop pellets (finish)
- 1   ounce Hallertauer whole hops (finish)
- 1   teaspoon gypsum
- 1   package Red Star lager yeast
- 3/4   cup Laaglander light dry malt extract to prime

- Original specific gravity: 1.076
- Terminal specific gravity: 1.018
- Age when judged (since bottling): 1 1/2 months

Melt In Your Mouth Creamy Porter

Lloyd Mower
Denver, Colorado
Second Place, Porter, 1988
(extract recipe)

Ingredients for 5 gallons

- 7   pounds Edme SFX dark malt extract

2 pounds crystal malt
4 ounces chocolate malt
4 ounces black patent malt
1 ounce Galena hops (60 minutes)
1/2 ounce Chinook hops (10 minutes)
1/2 ounce Chinook hops (2 minutes)
1 teaspoon Irish moss (last 15 minutes)
1 teaspoon gypsum
2 packets Munton & Fison ale yeast
1/2 cup corn sugar

- Original specific gravity: 1.048
- Terminal specific gravity: 1.024
- Age when judged (since bottling): 3 months

Judges' comments:
"Very attractive color, clear, good head. Could use more malty sweet finish. Use more crystal and maybe a little more roast grains."

"Big fruity, spicy hoppiness like a wheat beer or very hoppy ale; estery. Black color, tan head, head and head retention OK, appears clear. Flavor is a little astringent and a little sweet. Hop flavor is appropriate. Roasted malt leaves a bit of a husky finish. Medium body. Overall a bit astringent with lots of roasted flavor, probably from too much black malt."

Pat's Porter

Gary Brown
Menduta Heights, Minnesota
First Place, Porter, 1988
(extract recipe)

Ingredients for 5 gallons
6 pounds John Bull light malt extract
1/2 pound crystal malt
1/4 pound black patent malt
1/4 pound malted wheat

 1 1/2 ounces Wasatch Ale hops (60 minutes)
  1/2 ounce East Kent Goldings hops (30 minutes)
  1/2 ounce Hallertauer hops (15 minutes)
  1/8 ounce Chinook hops (45 minutes steep after boil)
   1 teaspoon brewer's salts
   1 teaspoon Irish moss
   2 packages Edme ale yeast
  3/4 cup corn sugar to prime

- Original specific gravity: 1.045
- Terminal specific gravity: 1.015
- Age when judged (since bottling): 1 1/2 months

Judges' comments
"Nice malt aroma. Try more roasted malt. Good appearance. The flavor has a nice balance but try more black patent or chocolate malt. I could drink a lot of this, however it needs more roasted malt flavor for category."

"Aroma is nicely balanced between hops and malt. Dark brown in appearance although a little light for the style. This beer lacks the roast grain flavor a porter should have, but it is very clean. It is somewhat inappropriate for the style but overall a well-made beer. I liked it very much."

Toluene Porter

Russell Schehrer
Boulder, Colorado
First Place, Porter, 1985
(mash/extract recipe)

Ingredients for 5 gallons
 6 1/2 pounds dark dry malt extract
   20 ounces Munich malt
   24 ounces crystal malt
   12 ounces dextrine (or Cara-pils) malt
   8 ounces black patent malt
 1 1/2 ounces Cascade boiling hops (1 hour)

3/4 ounce Cascade hops (last minute)
  2 teaspoons gypsum
     pinch of Irish moss
     Great Dane ale yeast
  1 teaspoon yeast energizer
1/2 cup corn sugar to prime

- Original specific gravity: 1.053
- Terminal specific gravity: 1.011
- Age when judged (since bottling): 8 1/2 months

Judges' comments

"Good malty aroma comes through without being harsh. Hops subtly nice—quite mellow. Good long, mellow aftertaste. Finishes well. Excellent effort."

"Nice, rich malty aroma with a hint of hops. Very good beer! Could find no defects, but it could use more head retention."

"Nice rich aroma. Hops powerful at first opening but mellow nicely. I find no fermentation defects—the balance would be hard to improve. This beer might win!"

"Beautiful hop aroma and excellent body. This beer was so tasty it reminded me of Sierra Nevada Porter."

SCOTCH ALE

Scotch Ale. A top-fermented beer of Scottish origin but now also produced in Belgium and France. It has an alcohol content of 7 or 8 percent by volume. Scotch ales are traditionally strong, very dark, thick and creamy. One particular example is brewed by Peter Maxwell Stuart in his castle at Traquair (20 miles south of Edinburgh). It is available on location from May to September. In Scotland, the pub expression for such a beer is "wee heavy," which also is the brand name of such an ale produced by Fowler.

Indian Scotch Ale

Dave Mela
Philadelphia, Pennsylvania
First Place, Scotch Ale, 1987
(extract recipe)

Ingredients for 4 1/2 gallons

3 1/3   pounds Munton & Fison "Premium" hopped malt
      extract syrup
   3   pounds Laaglander dry malt extract
1 1/2   pounds brown sugar
   2   teaspoons gypsum
   1   teaspoon salt
   1   teaspoon Irish moss
   2   ounces oak chips
1 1/2   teaspoons gelatin finings
 1/2   ounce Northern Brewer pellet hops (30 minutes)
 1/4   ounce Cascade pellet hops (30 minutes)
 1/2   ounce Fuggles leaf hops (steeped 10 minutes)
 1/2   Goldings leaf hops (steeped 10 minutes)
   1   package Muntona yeast
 1/4   teaspoon dextrose per bottle to prime

- Original specific gravity: 1.055
- Terminal specific gravity: 1.013
- Age when judged (since bottling): 5 1/2 months

Brewer's specifics

Oak chips were boiled in water five minutes, then steeped 20 minutes. The oak-chip water was strained onto the gelatin and all added to the fermenter one week prior to bottling.

Judges' comments

"Good malt nose, no hop nose. Good head retention, good carbonation. Pretty color. Good hop-malt balance, a little too much oak comes through. Great appearance, good balance."

"Slightly sweet, malty aroma. Very appropriate. Crystal clear, appropriate color. Good tight, long-lasting head. Tonic astringency from oak chips makes this ale pleasantly unique, but leaves a good effort slightly unbalanced (astringency dominates)."

Pacific Scotch Ale
Rod Romanak
Kailua-Kona, Hawaii
First Place, Scotch Ale, 1988
(extract recipe)

Ingredients for 5 gallons
- 8 pounds Munton & Fison amber malt extract syrup
- 1 pound crystal malt
- 1 ounce Chinook hops (45 minutes)
- 1/2 ounce Perle hops (10 minutes)
- 1 ounce Fuggles hops (after boil)
- 2 packages Muntona yeast
- 1/2 dextrose to prime

- Original specific gravity: 1.056
- Terminal specific gravity: 1.013
- Age when judged (since bottling): 3 months

Judges' comments
"Nice clean malt aroma. Beautiful clear mahogany, great carbonation, very good head retention. Wonderful, warm, mouth-filling malt flavor. This is great, clean, gorgeous, malty."

"Nice aroma, clean. Beautiful color, lovely creamy head. The flavor is well balanced, though perhaps a bit oxidized. A well-made beer. A fine example of the class. Congratulations."

Stumbling Penguins
Ralph Colaizzi
Pittsburgh, Pennsylvania
Second Place, Scotch Ale, 1988
(mash/extract recipe)

Ingredients for 5 gallons
- 3 1/3 pounds Bermaline malt extract
- 3 pounds light dry malt extract
- 1/2 pound dextrine malt

1/2 pound crystal malt
1/2 pound Munich malt
1 ounce Cluster hops (60 minutes)
1/4 ounce Cascade pellet hops (20 minutes)
1/4 ounce Nugget pellet hops (20 minutes)
1/2 ounce Cascade pellet hops (2 minutes)
1/4 ounce Nugget pellet hops (2 minutes)
1 pound brown sugar
Brewer's Choice "Chico Ale" yeast slurry (from previous batch)
3/4 cup dextrose

- Original specific gravity: 1.056
- Terminal specific gravity: 1.018
- Age when judged (since bottling): 2 months

Brewer's specifics
Mashed grains in 2 1/2 quarts water at 155 for 70 minutes. All added water had been boiled and then chilled.

Judges' comments
"Good aroma for category. Good color and clarity. Non-hop astringency comes through in aftertaste. Extremely drinkable. More malt would make heavier. I like this very much — balance is quite delicate. Fine job!"
"Sweet aroma, floral, warm alcoholic nose. Husky and astringent causes edge to maltiness."

Loch Ness Ale
Irvin Byers
Chicago, Illinois
Third Place, Scotch Ale, 1988
(all-grain recipe)

Ingredients for 7 gallons
5 1/2 pounds Briess 6-row malt
4 1/2 pounds English 2-row malt
1 1/2 pounds dextrine malt

1/2 pound crystal malt
  1 ounce Fuggles hops (60 minutes)
  1 ounce Cluster hops (60 minutes)
1/2 ounce Cascade hops (60 minutes)
1/2 ounce Cascade hops (at end of boil)
  1 pound dark brown sugar
  1 packet Burton salts
  2 packets Red Star ale yeast
1/2 cup corn sugar

- Original specific gravity: 1.054
- Terminal specific gravity: 1.016
- Age when judged (since bottling): 3 months

Brewer's specifics
  Mash at 95 degrees F for 15 minutes, 135 degrees F for 30 minutes, 155 degrees F for 60 minutes. Mash off at 175 degrees F. Sparge with 8 gallons of 175 degree F water. Primed with 50 ounces of wort and 1/2 cup of corn sugar.

Judges' comments
  "Buttery, rich aroma. Thick, creamy head. Flavor not sweet enough for the style. Very light, mild example—pleasant. Good drinkability."
  "Slightly phenolic aroma. Good head, although started out overcarbonated. Nice color. Flavor a little thin, but a very good effort. Nice malt/hop balance. Use more malt to beef up body. Finish is lacking complexity of malty/sweet. Salty/minerally."

Mt. Hood Ale

David W. Logsdon
Troutdale, Oregon
First Place, Scotch Ale, 1984
(all-grain recipe)

Ingredients for 4 1/2 gallons
  9 pounds pale barley malt

    1   pound roasted malt (home roasted — 275 degrees F for 2 hours)
1/2 ounce Brewers Gold (boiling hops, 55 minutes)
1/2 ounce Cascade (finishing hops, 10 minutes)
1/2 ounce Cascade (5 minutes)
  50 milliliters liquid ale yeast from stock culture

- Original specific gravity: 1.060
- Terminal specific gravity: 1.012
- Age when judged (since bottling): 3 months

Brewer's specifics

Mashing specifics: 3 1/2 gallons water; 30 minutes at 110 to 120 degrees F; 30 minutes at 130 to 140 degrees F; 60 minutes at 145 to 155 degrees F.

Sparge with 2 1/2 gallons at 160 degrees F over 20 minutes. Ferment at 65 degrees F for 4 weeks, 46 degrees F for 6 weeks.

Judges' comments

"Pleasant color, very nice head retention; nice clarity with some floaters. Great bready, doughy nose. Grapefruity ester maltiness in taste. Very nice effort — a winner and really on the right track. Cheers and brew on!"

"Slightly off smell — are the hops old?"

"Good balance in the aroma. An underlying malt sweetness in aftertaste. Good sound beer. Tended to be a little too sweet in aftertaste although there is a bitterness in the initial taste."

STOUT

Dry and Sweet Stout. In Britain, a very dark and very heavy top-fermented beer made from pale malt and 7 to 10 percent roasted, unmalted barley, often with the addition of caramel malt or sugar. Stout was first introduced by Guinness as an Extra Stout (higher gravity) version of their Plain Porter. The new stout was darker, richer, hoppier and more alcoholic than porter, which it gradually overtook in popularity until porter disappeared completely.

Today, a distinction is drawn between sweet and dry stout. Although both are highly hopped (600 to 700 grams per hectoliter), sweet stout is less bitter than the dry version.

Their alcohol content is about 5 percent by volume. Sweet stout is the English version of stout as opposed to the dry stout of Ireland. It has a slightly lactic flavor and is less alcoholic than dry stout. Sweet stout, also called milk stout, is typified by Mackeson. Dry stout is typified by Guinness Extra Stout.

Russian or Imperial Stout. In Britain, a very strong stout originally brewed from 1780 to World War I, by the London-based Anchor Brewery (now part of the Courage Corp.) for exportation as a winter warmer to St. Petersburg in Czarist Russia. Present-day Russian stout, brewed by Courage, is non-pasteurized and matured in casks for two months, then bottle-aged for one full year before it is marketed. It is brewed from an original wort gravity of 1.102 (25.5 degrees Balling) and contains 7.0 to 10.5 percent alcohol by volume. It is strong, dark copper-colored to black, and extremely rich. It has a strong bouquet and barley taste with fruity characteristics.

Because of its high gravity and its fruity flavor, Russian stout is more properly called barley wine.

Batch No. 260
Gary Zazkowski
San Jose, California
First Place, Dry Stout, 1982
(extract recipe)

Ingredients for 6 gallons
- 6 2/3 pounds John Bull plain dark malt extract
- 3 pounds dark dry malt extract
- 2 pounds black patent malt (cracked)
- 8 ounces British Northern Brewers whole hops

ale yeast
3/4   cup corn sugar for bottling

- Original gravity will be about 1.065.
- Terminal specific gravity will be about 1.020.

Brewer's specifics
Boil hops and malt with 2 gallons water for one hour.
Sparge into primary fermenter. Add cold water for 6 gallons total. Add yeast when temperature is below 78 degrees F.
Proceed with secondary fermentation and then bottle with corn sugar when fermentation is complete (2 to 4 weeks).

Kelly Irish Stout Ale

Steve Crossan
Niwot, Colorado
First Place, Dry Stout, 1980
(extract recipe)

Ingredients for 6 1/2 gallons
8   pounds Edme Irish Stout Hopped Ale Wort
2   ounces Cascade hops
Great Dane ale yeast
yeast nutrient (per instructions)
1 1/2   cups bottling sugar

- Original specific gravity: 1.045
- Terminal specific gravity: 1.013
- Age when judged (since bottling): 13 months

Brewer's specifics
Boil the Edme hopped wort with Cascade hops along with 2 gallons of water for 1 to 2 hours. Sparge. Add enough water to make 7 gallons in the primary fermenter. Add nutrient and yeast when temperature is about 72 degrees F. Rack into secondary at

1.020. This particular winning batch was kept in the secondary for 21 days and then bottled when fermentation was completed at 1.013.

Moon Shadow

Phil Anderson
Suttons Bay, Michigan
First Place, Dry Stout, 1985
(extract recipe)

Ingredients for 6 gallons
- 2 1/5 pounds Mountmellick Irish stout malt extract
- 3 1/3 pounds Laaglander Irish stout malt extract
- 3 pounds Munton and Fison dark dry malt extract
- 1/4 pound black patent malt
- 1/4 pound crystal malt
- 1/8 pound chocolate malt
- 1/8 pound roasted barley
- 3/4 ounce Fuggle leaf, 3/4 ounce Boullion leaf and 3/4 ounce Hallertauer leaf hops (1 hour)
- 1/4 ounce Fuggle leaf, 1/4 ounce Boullion leaf and 1/4 ounce Hallertauer leaf hops (5 minutes)
- 9 1/2 grams Burton water salts
- 1 clove star anise
- 1 teaspoon Irish moss
- 1 cup corn sugar to prime

- Original specific gravity: 1.056
- Terminal specific gravity: 1.016
- Age when judged (since bottling): 2 months

Judges' comments
"Nicely colored head with good "staying" quality. Smooth aroma, but not distinctive. Well-balanced flavor with a good hop finish."

"Not a powerful aroma; the flavor is nice, but the body a little thin. Nice finishing hops and aftertaste, well blended."

Nursing Stout No. 1

Frank Morris
Boulder, Colorado
Third Place, Sweet Stout, 1982
(extract recipe)

Ingredients for 6 1/2 gallons

    2 cans (7 pounds total) Edme Superbrew Stout kits
  3/4 pound dark dry malt
    3 pounds crystal malt
  1/3 pound roasted barley
  1/8 cup black patent malt
  1/4 cup blackstrap molasses
    1 ounce Hallertauer hop pellets
  1/4 ounce Cascade hop pellets
  1/4 ounce Bullion hop pellets
    1 ounce Cascade leaf hops
  1/4 cup gypsum
    1 teaspoon plain salt
    8 gallons distilled water
    2 packages ale yeast supplied with Edme kits

- Original gravity: 1.036 at 84 degrees F

Brewer's specifics

Bring to boil with two gallons of water: the grains, molasses, gypsum, salt and dry malt. Simmer for 35 minutes. Add malt extract syrup from cans, bring to a rolling boil, and add all hop pellets after 50 minutes of continued boiling. Add Cascade hops during the last five minutes of boiling. Cease boiling and let cool for 45 minutes. Sparge with remaining water.

Add ale yeast and pursue primary and secondary fermentation. When fermentation is complete, rack, add one heaping cup corn sugar and bottle.

Oatmeal Wheat Stout

Kenneth Kramer
Allentown, Pennsylvania
Second Place, Specialty Beers, 1985
(mash/extract recipe)

Ingredients for 5 gallons
- 3 pounds 2-row malted barley
- 1 pound wheat malt
- 2 pounds crystal malt
- 1 pound rolled oats
- 1 teaspoon diastatic enzyme powder in mash
- 2 1/2 cups roasted barley
- 4 cups black patent malt
- 3 1/3 pounds Edme Irish stout extract
- 3 1/3 pounds Edme light extract
- 1 stick brewer's licorice
- 1 ounce Tettnanger (45 minutes)
- 1/2 ounce Hallertauer (30 minutes)
- 2 ounces Hallertauer (last 2 minutes)
- 1/2 teaspoon Irish moss
- 1 packet Edme kit yeast
- 3/4 cup corn sugar to prime

- Original specific gravity: 1.078
- Terminal specific gravity: 1.032
- Age when judged (since bottling): 2 months

Judges' comments
"Good stout aroma, the grains come through. The flavor has real character."

"Good crisp aroma. Excellent flavor — lingering sweetness balancing the harshness."

"Nice creamy head. Aroma is very faintly medicinal — it may have been the brewer's licorice. A nice oatmeal type stout with clean flavor, a very good beer!"

Light Antithesis
Otto Zavaton
Boulder, Colorado
First Place, Stout, 1979
(all-grain recipe)

This recipe is for 30 gallons, but one may choose to brew a smaller batch. There is no reason why this recipe can't be brewed in a lesser quantity. For the record, we're publishing the recipe exactly as it was brewed.

Ingredients for 30 gallons
- 70 pounds pale malted barley (grain form)
- 7 pounds roasted barley
- 17 ounces Cascade hops
- 6 cups corn sugar for bottling
- 3 tablespoons ascorbic acid
  water

- Original specific gravity: 1.060
- Final specific gravity: 1.017

Brewer's specifics
The malted barley and roasted barley were mashed for 2 hours. Using the "infusion" method of mashing, 18 gallons of water at about 165-170 degrees F were mixed with the cracked malt and barley, effectively bringing the temperature down to 152 degrees. It is important to keep the stiff porridge-like mash at 152 degrees F for 2 hours, after which the mash is agitated and then sparaged. The "liquor" was then brought to boiling for 2 hours with the addition of 9 ounces of the hops. Half way through boiling, 6 more ounces of the hops were added. During the final 5 minutes, the remaining 2 ounces were thrown in.

The wort was then sparged and water added to make a total of 30 gallons.

The brew was racked. Six cups of corn sugar and 3 tablespoons of ascorbic acid were added, mixed well and Light Antithesis was bottled.

Imperial Stout

Mark Stankiewicz
Norwich, Connecticut
First Place, Stout, 1987
(extract recipe)

Ingredients for 5 gallons
6 2/3 pounds John Bull unhopped malt extract syrup
3 1/3 pounds Edme dark hopped malt extract syrup
    2 pounds Munton & Fison light dry malt extract
    2 pounds pale malt
    1 pound crystal malt
    1 pound black patent malt
    1 cup honey
    1 cup molasses
    1 licorice stick
2 1/2 ounces Bullion hops (60 minutes)
    2 ounces Fuggles hops (60 minutes)
    1 ounce Cascade hops (60 minutes)
    1 ounce Cascade hops (2 minutes)
    2 packages Red Star ale yeast
    1 package Champagne yeast
  3/4 cup dextrose to prime

* Original specific gravity: 1.107
* Terminal specific gravity: 1.035
* Age when judged (since bottling): 6 months

Judges' comments
   "A slight estery nose, no hop or malt aroma. A very black, clean brew, with a nice creamy head. The fruity character is overdone, almost winey—very sweet. I don't sense enough malt flavor. This brew is reasonably true to style. It is enjoyable to drink."
   "Aroma not spectacular; OK, but could be more interesting. Definitely underhopped in both taste and bouquet. Alcoholic! Almost barley-wine taste. Good job, could be even better if just slightly drier and hoppier. Good example of a sweet Imperial stout. Thank you! You will make the finals!"

Jerry Lee Lewis

Byron Burch
Santa Rosa, California
First Place, Russian Imperial Stout, 1986
(mash/extract recipe)

Ingredients for 5 gallons
5 pounds Munton & Fison extra dark dry malt extract
3 1/3 pounds John Bull plain dark malt syrup
1 pound crystal malt
4 ounces Munich malt (mashed)
8 ounces black patent malt (finely ground and boiled 30 minutes)
5 pounds Great Fermentations white rice syrup
1 pound corn sugar
2 3/4 ounces Northern Brewer pellets and 1/4 ounce Cluster pellets (60 minutes)
1 3/4 ounces Nugget pellets and 1/4 ounce Eroica pellets (30 minutes)
2 ounces Cascade pellets and 1/4 ounce Saaz pellets (dry hopped for aroma)
10 grams Red Star Pasteur Champagne wine yeast
1/2 teaspoon Great Fermentations nutrient
3/4 cup corn sugar (syrup) and 5 ounces lactose to prime

- Original specific gravity: 1.099
- Terminal specific gravity: 1.040
- Age when judged (since bottling): 6 1/2 months

Judges' comments
"This head does not quit—Linda Lovelace prime this sucker? Russki Imperial Stout! Phew—what planet can hold this beer? Talk about an immense, intense, luscious, voluptuous brew."

"Ahhh—what a nice hop aroma. Surprisingly sweet for a strong stout. Cleanly brewed. Very drinkable. Definitely needs more alcohol for category."

"Looks like a Russian Imperial Stout, corner of glass is clear! Lovely hop aroma, hint of chocolate malt. Very full, very balanced, nicely aged and mellow. Keep this up!"

WHEAT BEER

Berliner Weisse. A regional beer of northern Germany, principally Berlin; a very pale (but not white) top-fermented beer of low-density (1.028 to 1.032, 7 to 8 degrees Balling) made from a one-to-three or -four wheat-to-barley ratio. It is lightly hopped and mildly alcoholic at 2 to 3 percent alcohol by weight (2.5 to 3.7 percent by volume). A secondary fermentation induced by the addition of a lactic acid culture (Lactobacillus, sour milk) at 20 degrees C (68 degrees F) is responsible for its dry, sharp flavor, thick white foam and the deposit of yeast in the bottle.

It is traditionally served in large, bowl-shaped stemglasses with a dash of green essence of woodruff or red raspberry syrup (*Schulthies Berliner Weisse* and *Kindel Berliner Weisse*). Its popularity dates back to Imperial Germany, but it is mentioned in texts as early as 1572.

Weizenbier. In Germany, a generic name for top-fermented wheat beers, especially those of the south (mainly Bavaria, Münich and Baden-Württemberg). They are sometimes called Süddeutsches Weizenbier to distinguish them from those produced in northern Germany, which are generally referred to as Berliner Weisse or simply Weissbier.

Compared to the northern Berliner Weisse, Weizenbier has a much higher wheat-to-barley ratio (1:1 to 2:1 as opposed to 1:3), a higher density (1.048 to 1.056 or 12 to 14 degrees Balling as opposed to 1.028 to 1.032, or 7 to 8 degrees Balling) and a higher alcohol content (+5 percent by volume as opposed to 3 to 4 percent). Weizen is also fuller flavored but less acid. It is bottle-conditioned and available in two forms: with yeast sediments (Weizen mit Hefe or Hefeweizen[bier]) or without (Hefefreiweizen[bier]). Both types are often preferred with a slice of lemon. In Bavaria, wheat beer also is known as Bayerischer Weize or Süddeutsches Weizenbier.

Dunkel (dark) Weizen. These are dark Weizen beers with substantial malty bodies and fruity palates. They tend to be fairly high in alcoholic content, and are sometimes referred to as Weizenbocks. They range from 5.0 to 6.5 percent alcohol by volume.

Weiss

Lucie Eckert
Wauwatosa, Wisconsin
First Place, Wheat Beer, 1985
(all-grain recipe)

Ingredients for 5 gallons
    5   pounds 6-row barley malt
3 1/2   pounds wheat malt

1/2 pound light caramel malt
1/2 ounce Hallertauer (10 percent) hop pellets
    Red Star ale yeast
3/4 cup corn sugar to prime

- Original specific gravity: 1.050
- Terminal specific gravity: 1.010
- Double-stage closed fermentation in glass at 55 to 60 degrees F for 2 weeks
- Age when judged (since bottling): 3 months

Brewer's specifics
    Add grains to 9 quarts water at 130 degrees F; stabilize at 120 to 122 for 30 minutes. Add 4 1/2 quarts boiling water, raise temperature to 154 to 156 and hold for 90 minutes. Sparge with 5 gallons water at 175 degrees F.

Judges' comments
    "Excellent clarity, good head. Appropriate fruity bouquet, a tad faint. Flavor is a bit heavy on the malt."
    "Smooth, creamy head, good retention. Nice bouquet and flavor balance. Quite a pleasing beer."

Big Tree Weizenbier

Ron Slaughter
Salida, Colorado
First Place, Wheat Beer, 1983
(extract recipe)

Ingredients for 6 gallons
3 1/3 pounds Munton & Fison amber plain extract
    3 pounds Munton & Fison light plain malt extract
    3 pounds wheat malt, crushed
1/2 teaspoon Koji concentrate
1 1/2 ounces Hallertauer pellets
    1 tablespoon gypsum
1/2 teaspoon kosher salt

1 package Muntona ale yeast
   wort for priming

* Original specific gravity: 1.052
* Terminal specific gravity: 1.010
* Approximate temperature of fermentation: 68 degrees F
* Age when entered (since bottling): 4 weeks

Brewer's specifics
   Mash the wheat malt with the Koji in 3 quarts water (pH 5.0) for
15 minutes at 130 degrees F.
   Sparge with 2 gallons of water, until liquor is no longer sweet.
Add extracts, gypsum and salt.
   Boil wort for 10 minutes and add 1 ounce Hallertauer pellets.
Continue boiling, and 10 minutes later add the other 1/2 ounce of
hops to finish. Cool wort and add water to make 6 gallons.
   Draw off 1 gallon of wort, cap it tightly and refrigerate for later
kraeusen/priming. Pitch the yeast. Ferment 3 weeks in carboys
with one racking after 3 days to help clearing. Add 7 pints of wort
to prime and bottle.

Wheat Beer No. 4

Gordon Olson
Los Alamos, New Mexico
First Place, Wheat Beer, 1987
(all-grain recipe)

Ingredients for 5 1/2 gallons
      6 pounds pale malt
 3 1/2 pounds wheat malt
      1 pound dextrin malt
      1 tablespoon gypsum (in mash)
   1/2 teaspoon Irish moss (30 minutes)
 1 1/2 ounces Cluster hops (90 minutes)
   1/2 ounce Cluster hops (30 minutes)
      2 packages Red Star ale yeast
   3/4 cup dextrose and 1/2 teaspoon vitamin C to prime

- Original specific gravity: 1.047
- Terminal specific gravity: 1.016
- Age when judged (since bottling): 2 1/2 months

Brewer's specifics
Mash in at 95 degrees F, slowly heating to 125 degrees F in 40 minutes. Add 1 gallon boiling water to get 150 degrees F. Heat to 155 degrees F and get starch conversion in 30 minutes. Wort chiller used after the boil.

Judges' comments
"Nice clovelike spicy aroma. Nice and clean. Very clear. Weak head for wheat beer. Bubbles are a bit large. Flavor a bit too bitter. Needs more clove-yeast taste. Nice clovelike aroma but lacks clove taste."
"Good clove nose. Some malt sweetness, bit of sourness. Faint yeastiness, more pronounced as it warms. Good! Scant head, very fine bubbles. Yellow gold. Clear but not brilliant. Well carbonated. Moderate head. Flavor has cloves present. Grainy fullness, not quite crisp and tart enough. Faintly tannic finish. Very good representative of style, a lot like Spaten Club-Weisse. Maybe oversparged?"

Wheat Bock No. 8
Harold L. Gee
Mesa, Arizona
Third Place, Wheat Beer, 1987
(Dunkel Weizen, Wiezen Bock)
(extract recipe)

Ingredients for 6 gallons
6 pounds Williams wheat malt extract syrup
3 1/5 pounds Specialty Products International Home Brew kit hopped malt extract
1/2 pound dark dry malt extract
1 pound pale malt
1 pound wheat malt

1/2　pound Munich malt
1/2　pound crystal malt
1/2　pound flaked wheat
1/4　pound chocolate malt
　2　ounces Burton brewing salts
1/2　ounce Perle hops (60 minutes)
1/2　ounce Saaz hops (30 minutes)
1/4　ounce Cascade hops (1 minute)
1/2　ounce Vierka dark Munich yeast
3/4　cup dextrose to prime

- Original specific gravity: 1.067
- Terminal specific gravity: 1.026
- Age when judged (since bottling): 3 1/2 months

Brewer's specifics
　　Mash: Add 2 1/2 gallons tap water of 120 degrees F to pale malt, wheat malt, Munich malt and flaked wheat. Bring to 130 degrees F, hold for 20 minutes. Bring slowly to 150 degrees F, hold for one hour. Bring to 155 degrees F and hold for 30 minutes. Steep crystal malt and chocolate malt in one gallon cold water. Bring slowly to a boil. Strain into wort when boil reached. Bring wort to a boil, add all extracts and Burton brewing salts.

Judges' comments
　　"Spicy wheat aroma, alcoholic. Color is dark brown with tinge of red, medium-dark tan head. Good head retention, good looking. Slightly roasty flavor. Alcoholic, wheat characteristics not obvious. Sweet malt flavor with full body. Overall a bit roasty with full body. Wheat not obvious. Good body, clean finish. A good beer."
　　"Aroma faint but in correct proportions. Deep reddish-brown color. Maybe a little too dark. The rich appealing malty taste tends to mask wheat character. I really like this beer even if it is a bit removed from the category."

BOCK

Bock. A very strong beer originally brewed by top fermentation in the Hanseatic League town of Einbeck in Lower Saxony where it is still brewed and known as Ur-Bock, the original bock. It was once a heavy dark beer brewed in winter for consumption in spring. German bock beers are now brewed by bottom fermentation and are usually dark brown, but pale bocks are increasing in popularity and a distinction is sometimes made between "light bock beer" and "dark bock beer." Modern bockbiers, according to German law, must be fermented from an original wort gravity of at least 1.064 (16 degrees Plato), resulting in an alcoholic content of 6 percent by weight or higher (7.5 percent by volume). They are full-bodied, malty and well-hopped.

Etym: From the town of Einbeck (circa 1250) in northern Germany.

This beer was later exported to Münich and was one of the first beers to be brewed by the Hofbraü, the brewery of the dukes of Bavaria. In the 18th century the name became Oanbock and was shortened to bock.

According to one legend, bock was first made from the dregs of barrels and vats at spring cleaning. This is obviously untrue since such a beer would have been weak, to say the least. Because the word bock also means male goat or billy goat in German, such an animal often is represented on the labels of bottles containing bockbier.

Bock beers first appeared in America around 1840 as seasonal beers available at springtime. After Prohibition was repealed (December 1933), bars proclaimed the good news with a sign saying "Bock is back." But in fact the sales of bock dwindled and production was discontinued until the 1970s when a few bock beers were revived. American bock beers are usually light-bodied and mildly hopped. The name of these so-called bock beers comes not from their strength, but rather from their dark color and artificial caramel flavoring.

In France, bock refers to a medium strength beer of medium density, ranging from 3.3 to 3.9 degrees Régie.

Doppelbock. In Germany, a beer much stronger than simple bock but not necessarily doubly so, as the German adjective doppel, meaning double, implies. According to German law, Doppelbock must be brewed from an original wort gravity of 1.072 (18 degrees Plato) to 1.120 (28 degrees Plato), resulting in a strength of 7.5 to 13 percent alcohol by volume.

The brand names of doppelbocks always end with the suffix –ator (Animator, Salvator, Optimator, Delicator, Maximator, Triumphator). The original of the style, named Salvator after the Saviour, was brewed by the Italian monks of the order of St. Francis of Paula, in Bavaria, during the Counter-Revolution period. They were granted permission to sell their product by the court of Bavaria in 1780. The monastic brewery is now operated by the privately owned Paulaner-Thomas-Braü.

Bock-in-the-Saddle (Again)
Tom Ayres
Boston, Massachusetts
Second Place, Bock, 1988
(extract recipe)

Ingredients for 5 gallons
6 2/3 pounds Munton & Fison light malt extract syrup
3 1/3 pounds Munton & Fison amber malt extract syrup
1 pound Munton & Fison light dry malt extract
1/2 pound toasted 2-row malted barley (350 degrees F for 10 minutes)
1/2 pound crystal malt
1/4 pound chocolate malt
3 inches Brewer's licorice (boiled with extracts)
1 ounce Chinook leaf hops (60 minutes)
2 ounces Hallertauer leaf hops (40 minutes)
1/2 ounce Tettnanger leaf hops (40 minutes)
1/2 ounce Tettnanger leaf hops (15 minutes)
1 teaspoon Irish moss
2 packages Red Star lager yeast
5/8 cup dextrose to prime

- Original specific gravity: 1.078 (estimated)
- Terminal specific gravity: 1.016
- Age when judged (since bottling): 5 months

Judges' comments
"Good nose, sweet, nice touch of hops. Very dark, clear, good head. Very smooth and drinkable. Nice carbonation, clean aftertaste. I like it."

"Nice colored head, golden and creamy. Not a lot of aromatics but it smells clean. Very subtle malt sweetness. The flavor is not as malty or distinct as I would like it, but what is there is OK. Warming. There's a subtle intensity about this brew. Brings out the malt character."

Tracey's First

Keith Wilbourn
Millers Falls, Massachusetts
First place, Bock, 1988
(extract recipe)

Ingredients for 5 gallons
    6 pounds Munton & Fison light dry malt extract
3 1/3 pounds John Bull amber unhopped malt extract syrup
  5/8 ounce Hallertauer hops (60 minutes)
  5/8 ounce Hallertauer hops (30 minutes)
  5/8 ounce Hallertauer hops (end of boil)
1 3/4 ounces Hallertauer hops (20 minutes steep after boil)
    1 package Wyeast Brewers Choice liquid lager yeast
        (No. 2007)
  2/3 cup cane sugar to prime

- Original specific gravity: 1.062-1.068
- Terminal specific gravity: unknown
- Age when judged (since bottling): 2 1/2 months

Judges' comments
    "Alcoholic aroma, but malt and hops are there. Perhaps a little hazy due to overcarbonation. Good malt sweetness. Would have liked just a bit more hops in taste, but still good! Slightly thin due to fermentation going too far. Close to dopplebock."
    "Aroma light, not quite enough malt for category. Appearance somewhat cloudy. Nice color. A little overcarbonated. Good flavor, a little light on malty sweetness."

Ehren Bock

Gary W. Schmidt
Webster Groves, Missouri
Second Place, Bock, 1987
(mash/extract recipe)

Ingredients for 5 gallons
    8   pounds Alexander light malt extract syrup
3 1/3   pounds Munton & Fison dark hopped malt extract
        syrup
  1/4   pound Munich malt
  1/4   pound chocolate malt
  1/8   pound black patent malt
    1   ounce Willamette whole hops (45 minutes)
    1   ounce Willamette whole hops (30 minutes)
    1   ounce Tettnanger whole hops (dry hopped in primary)
    2   packages Red Star lager yeast
        Kraeusened, 1 package Vierka lager yeast and 3/4 cup
        dextrose to prime

- Original specific gravity: 1.065
- Terminal specific gravity: 1.014
- Age when judged (since bottling): 1 1/2 months

Brewer's specifics
    Munich malt mashed at 122 degrees F for 15 minutes. Then 155 degrees F for 30 minutes. Strain, then place in kettle with other grains. Add three gallons water, bring to boil, remove grains. Add extract, boil for 75 minutes. Strain into primary over hops in bag, cool to 70 degrees F. Pitch 3/4 gallon yeast starter (started two days prior with 2 packages yeast and 1 cup dry malt). Ferment at 60 degrees F until racking gravity is reached (one week). Rack into secondary. Lager at 40 to 45 degrees F for five weeks. Finish ferment at 60 degrees F (one week). Rack to primary, kraeusen, and bottle.

Judges' comments
    "Smells a bit bready-yeasty. Malt is very nice. Nice reddish

color. Perfect creamy head. Good alcohol. Very nice balance of sweet-bitter-dryness and alcohol."

"Malt aroma comes through well. Good clarity and color. Head retention is fair. Very full flavor, hop character well in evidence, but not overstrong. One of the best I've tasted in this category. Good work!"

Hansbock

John Judd and Don Hoag
Duluth, Minnesota
First Place, Traditional German Bock, 1985
(all-grain recipe)

Ingredients for 5 gallons
- 7   pounds 6-row lager malt
- 2   pounds Munich malt
- 8   ounces crystal malt
- 5   ounces dextrin malt
- 5   ounces chocolate malt
- 2   ounces black malt
- 1/2 ounce Tettnanger leaf hops (1 hour)
- 1/2 ounce Hallertauer hop pellets (1 hour)
- 1/2 ounce Hallertauer hops (15 minutes)
- 1/2 ounce Tettnanger leaf (end of boil, steep for 10 to 15 minutes)
- 1   teaspoon Irish moss
- 1   packet Red Star lager yeast
- 3/4 cup corn sugar to prime

- Original specific gravity: 1.049
- Terminal specific gravity: 1.012
- Double-stage fermentation in glass at 50 to 55 degrees F for 3 weeks
- Age when judged (since bottling): 2 1/2 months

Brewer's specifics
Mash all the malts at 155 degrees F for 1 1/2 hours.

Judges' comments
"Nice 'ur-bock' appearance; good head retention. A bit hazy—
protein haze. Pleasant hop aroma and good flavor."

Old Fort Worth Bock
J. C. Martin, C. C. Martin, C. R. Grimes
Euless, Texas
First Place, Bock, 1986
(all-grain recipe)

Ingredients for 10 gallons
21 pounds 2-row Klages malt
3 pounds crystal malt
1 pound black patent malt
2 1/2 ounces Cascade hop pellets (boil, 90 minutes)
2 1/4 ounces Styrian Goldings leaf hops (finish, 60 minutes)
1/2 teaspoon Epsom salts to sparge water
1 cup (slurry) Weihenstephan #308 yeast
primed by kraeusening to raise S.G. by 0.004

- Original specific gravity: 1.063
- Terminal specific gravity: 1.014
- Age when judged (since bottling): 2 1/2 months

Brewer's specifics
1 1/2 hours infusion mash, sparge until 10 gallons collected.
Filtered two weeks before bottling under counter-pressure.

Judges' comments
"Color almost too dark, nice clarity, overall good appearance
but head could be nicer. Deep butterscotchy aroma with malt and
alcohol coming through. Hops are a little light, very clean with appropriate sweetness, pleasing. Quite good, pleasant, enjoyable."
"Beautiful head but maybe overcarbonated, slightly dark. Good
malt-hop balance. Slight oxidized taste. Very enjoyable beer —
good job. Oxidation may be from age."

"Super clarity in this beer; very creamy head; also very large; possibly too much; color is too dark. Lighten up on dark grains. Very malty with alcohol complexity; nice balance. Very nice malt sweetness that really lingers on the tongue; could use a little more. Good body for the amount of malt and alcohol present. I could drink a lot of this. Go a little lighter on the dark grains next time and this will be a winner!"

Doppelbock

Steve Crossan
Galesburg, Illinois
First Place, Doppelbock, 1984
(mash/extract recipe)

Ingredients for 5 gallons
3 1/4   pounds pale malted barley
  2/3   pound pale malted barley toasted for 10 minutes at 350 degrees F
  10   ounces Munich malt
    6   ounces crystal malt
    6   ounces chocolate malt
    5   ounces black patent malt
  10   ounces dextrine malt
  10   pounds dark dry malt extract
1 1/2   ounces Bullion hops (boil 1 1/4 hours)
  2/3   ounce Fuggle hops (boil 15 minutes)
  4/5   ounce Saaz hops (add at end of boil)
    8   ounces yeast slurry cultured from a previous batch
  3/4   cup corn sugar to prime

• Original specific gravity: 1.074

Brewer's specifics
Add 6 quarts water at 130 degrees F to the grains. Hold at 110 to 115 degrees F for 30 minutes. Add 3 quarts boiling water to raise the temperature to 142 degrees. Raise to 150 and hold 15 minutes,

raise to 158 and hold 15 minutes. Sparge to a gravity of 1.020 and continue by adding extract and boiling wort.

Judges' comments
"Appropriate deep, dark color. A definite malt taste in the aroma, but somewhat faint. Doppelbock style — well done for the type. Slight husky taste in the finish, but on the whole a very creditable effort."

"Somewhat on the dark side for German bock. I like the nose balance but could use more hoppy aroma. Good malty sweetness in the taste; slightly excessive bitter — excessive hops. For an extract brew the malty flavor is done well." (Editor's note: The judges don't see the recipes.)

Konsumator

Lt. Col. Charles F. Smith
Kaiserslautern, Germany
First Place, Doppelbock, 1987
(mash/extract recipe)

Ingredients for 5 gallons
  9 pounds dry malt extract
  3 pounds Munich malt
  2 pounds Klages 2-row pale malt
  1 pound crystal malt
  1 pound chocolate malt
  1/2 pound rolled wheat
  1/2 pound dextrine malt
  1 teaspoon gypsum
  2 1/2 ounces Hallertauer hops (5 1/2-ounce infusions from 105 minutes to 60 minutes)
  2 ounces Hallertauer hops (in hop back)
  2 packages Old Danish lager yeast
  1/2 package yeast and 1 cup dry extract to prime (kraeusening)

- Original specific gravity: 1.085
- Terminal specific gravity: 1.029
- Age when judged (since bottling): 2 months

Brewer's specifics
   Mashed by double decoction.

CONTINENTAL DARK

Continental Dark. Primarily a product of the German brewing tradition. These dark lagers have less sweetness, more hops and carbonation than their brown ale counterparts. They are characterized by a clean, subtle, crisp delicateness that can only be obtained by a significant period of cold storage. 4.0 to 4.8 percent alcohol by volume.

Eigen Dunkelbier

Barry Miller
Salt Lake City, Utah
First Place, Continental Dark, 1986
(extract recipe)

Ingredients for 6 1/2 gallons
    7   pounds Edme DMS malt extract syrup
2 1/5   pounds Premier dark hopped malt extract syrup
    1   pound crystal malt
    1   pound chocolate malt
  1/4   pound black patent malt
    1   ounce Cascade hops (60 minutes)
    1   ounce Hallertauer hops (60 minutes)
    1   ounce Saaz hops (60 minutes)
    1   ounce Saaz hops (15 minutes)
    2   packages Red Star lager yeast
    1   cup Munton & Fison light dry malt extract to prime

- Original specific gravity: none taken
- Terminal specific gravity: about 1.014
- Age when judged (since bottling): 7 months

Brewer's specifics
    Grains steeped 45 minutes in 120-degree-F water and "sparged" into boil pot. Concentrated wort added to cool water in plastic pail to allow precipitation of trub. Racked off trub to glass carboy and brought to full volume. Yeast pitched and set to ferment at about 38 degrees F. Racked to clean fermenter at 2 weeks. Bottled at 8 weeks. Storage at 38 degrees F.

Judges' comments
    "Beautiful red-brown color. Very clean, nice creamy head. Malty aroma with some hop complement. I could drink a lot of this. Sweet but with a good balance. Body slightly heavy for category."
    "Good head, holds well. Aroma correct, good balance. Small faults but widespread. Balance seems off a little."
    "Thick, gorgeous head shows use of enough malt. Basically

smooth and continental with a minimum of hops.   Fine for a
continental dark. Smooth and drinkable but more hops would be
welcome here."

Holiday Special

Michael Gatschet
Lakewood, Colorado
First Place, Continental Dark, 1985
(mash/extract recipe)

Ingredients for 5 gallons
- 3 1/3 pounds Munton and Fison light malt extract
- 3 1/3 pounds Munton and Fison amber malt extract
- 1 pound light dry extract
- 3/4 pound crystal malt
- 1 1/4 pounds Munich malt — mash
- 1 cup roasted barley
- 1 ounce Cascade hops (8.5 alpha), 1 ounce Willamette (6.5 alpha) (1 hour)
- 3/4 ounce Cascade hops (at end)
- 1/4 teaspoon antioxident
- 1 packet Red Star lager yeast
- 3/4 cup corn sugar to prime

- Original specific gravity: 1.048
- Terminal specific gravity: 1.013
- Age when judged (since bottling): 8 months

Brewer's specifics
Steep grains for 1 hour at 135 to 150 degrees F.

Judges' comments
"Malty aroma, seems to lack hops considerably. Hops come
through as part of an alcohol taste. Woody. Nice follow-through,
good beer."
"Color is a little light. Nutty aroma; Scotch-to-cognac smell;

low in hop aromatics. Malt/hop balance varied more toward malt. Aftertaste is a long hoppy bitterness. Hops come through only on bitterness. Resembles a nut ale aroma."

Midnite Lager
J.A. Morris
Victoria, Texas
First Place, Continental Dark, 1985
(all-grain recipe)

Ingredients for 5 gallons
- 7 1/2 pounds pale malt
- 2 1/2 pounds crystal malt
- 1/2 pound flaked barley
- 1 1/2 ounces Northern Brewer hops (45 minutes)
- 1 ounce Hallertauer hops (end of boil)
- 1/2 ounce Hallertauer hops (dry hop)
- 2 teaspoons calcium carbonate
   Budweiser lager yeast starter
- 1 1/4 cups corn sugar in 2 cups wort to prime

- Original specific gravity: 1.048
- Terminal specific gravity: 1.011
- Single-stage fermentation in glass at 45 degrees F for 6 weeks
- Age when judged (since bottling): 5 1/2 weeks

Brewer's specifics
Mash for 30 minutes at 131 degrees F; 60 minutes at 151 degrees F. Sparge with 2 1/2 gallons of hot distilled water.

Judges' comments
"Nice roasted color, dark for the category. Aroma stands out as a robust German lager; hops are delicate but very appealing. Noticeable malt sweetness but not overpowering, with a long aftertaste."

"Aroma is mild on hops and malt, but balanced. Nice woody, hoppy flavor; good balance and finish."

"Lack of hop and malt nose. Hop/malt is nicely balanced in the flavor; body holds to aftertaste. Lacks crisp flavor clarity of the Continental Dark category though it's well brewed — possibly give more attention to maltiness and to temperature of fermentation."

Troll House Brown Lager

Mary Frances Richardson
St. Catharines, Ontario, Canada
First Place, Continental Dark, 1987
(all-grain recipe)

Ingredients for 6 gallons

4	pounds 2-row malted barley
2 1/2	pounds 6-row malted barley
2 1/2	pounds whole rice
1	teaspoon gypsum
1/2	ounce Cascade hops (60 minutes)
1/2	ounce Hersbrucker hops (60 minutes)
1/4	ounce Saaz hops (60 minutes)
1/8	ounce Cascade hops (20 minutes)
1/16	ounce Saaz hops (20 minutes)
1/8	ounce Hersbrucker hops (20 minutes)
1/8	ounce Hallertauer hops (20 minutes)
1/16	ounce Cascade hops (2 minutes)
1/16	ounce Saaz hops (2 minutes)
1/16	ounce Hersbrucker hops (2 minutes)
1/16	ounce Hallertauer hops (2 minutes)
2	packages Red Star lager yeast
7/8	cup dextrose to prime

- Original specific gravity: 1.047
- Terminal specific gravity: 1.012
- Age when judged (since bottling): 2 1/2 months

Judges' comments

"Clean, delicate, almost faint, hop and malt bouquet. Appearance almost brilliant, very active head, a bit orange in color. Smooth body, malt sweetness nicely balanced by hops. Could use a little more toasty malt flavor. Really nice beer. A winner. Keep up the good work."

"Aroma of maltiness with hops. Dark golden color, light head with good retention, clear, maybe slight haze. Slightly alcoholic, lots of hops at the beginning, light to medium body, malty finish with hoppy bitterness. Clean, light, medium body. I could drink a lot of this. Good beer, maybe a little sweet."

EXPORT

Export/Dortmunder. A blond or gold-colored, bottom-fermented beer from Dortmund (Westphalia), Germany's largest brewing city. Although the brewing rights of that city were granted by imperial decree in 1293, the Dortmund style beer was not introduced until the 1840s. The original of this style is often symbolized by the acronym DAB, which stands for Dortmunder Aktien Brauerei and is better known locally as Export because it was once brewed for exporting.

Outside Germany, in Belgium and Holland, for example,

beers brewed in this style are often called Dort. In style it is intermediate between Pilsener and Münchener, darker and less bitter (200 to 220 grams/hectoliter of hops as opposed to 400 to 500 grams/hectoliter in Pilsener) than the first and drier. It is also less malty (180 to 200 grams/hectoliter of hops in Münchener) and paler than the second, and slightly stronger than both, containing 4.2 percent alcohol by weight or 5.2 percent by volume.

Ehren Export

Gary W. Schmidt
Warson Woods, Missouri
First Place, Export, 1988
(extract recipe)

Ingredients for 5 gallons

4	pounds Alexanders light unhopped malt extract syrup
3	pounds Munton & Fison light unhopped dry malt extract
1/4	pound malted barley
1/8	pound crystal malt
1/8	pound wheat malt
1	ounce roasted barley
1	ounce Hallertauer hops (75 minutes)
1	ounce Cascade hops (60 minutes)
1/2	ounce Bullion hops (45 minutes)
1/2	ounce Hallertauer hops (30 minutes steep after boil)
1/4	ounce Saaz hops (30 minutes steep after boil)
1	teaspoon gypsum
1	package Burton water salts
	Liquid lager yeast starter
1	cup dextrose to prime

- Original specific gravity: 1.052
- Terminal specific gravity: 1.015
- Age when judged (since bottling): 6 months

Brewer's specifics
   Add grains to water. Bring to a boil and remove grains. Add hops as above. Add extracts last 20 minutes of boil only. Ferment at 50 degrees F for 10 to 14 days, then 40 to 45 degrees F for 45 to 60 days.

Judges' comments
   "Some light flowery hop aroma, but mostly malty. Clear but not brilliant, golden color, nice head with good retention, tiny bubbles. Thin watery body, a clean hoppy finish. No off-flavors. It urges me to have another sip. I would prefer a bit more hop bouquet and a bit more malt. The carbonation is OK. Overall, a good beer."
   "Aroma inoffensive — not much comes through. Appearance appropriate for style, but at the darkest end. Malt comes through in the flavor. Not much hop to back up aftertaste, though phenolic aroma is slight."

Regal Dixie
Al Haydel
New Orleans, Lousiana
First Place, Export, 1983
(mash/extract recipe)

Ingredients for 5 gallons
   5 pounds light dry malt extract
   4 pounds lager malt (cracked)
   3 ounces Fuggles hop pellets (bittering)
   1 ounce Cascade leaf hops (aromatic)
   2 teaspoons non-iodized salt
   1 teaspoon Irish moss
      Lager yeast
   1 cup corn sugar

- Original specific gravity: 1.055
- Terminal specific gravity: 1.019

Brewer's specifics

In 2 gallons of water, mash the grains at 160 degrees F for 1 hour. Sparge and add to brewing liquor: dry malt extract, bittering hops and salt. Boil for 45 minutes. Add Irish moss and continue boil for 15 minutes. Add aromatic hops and boil for 15 minutes, then remove from heat.

Sparge with cold water to 5 gallons and pitch yeast. Rack to secondary after 5 days. When fermentation is complete, add corn sugar for priming and bottle.

Judges' comments

"Nice hoppy nose, clarity, head. Crisp grain, clean and balanced, with just a bit of excess bitterness. Nice job!"

"Good hop nose, crisply bitter, good, perhaps too much. Very good effort. I could drink this a long time!"

Dutch Style Lager
Dave Miller
St. Louis, Missouri
First place, Light Lagers, Best of Show, 1981
(all-grain recipe)

Ingredients for 5 gallons
9 gallons soft, neutral water (9 quarts mash and 5 gallons sparge, rest in reserve)
5 1/2 pounds lager malt
1 1/2 pounds rice
1 1/2 teaspoons or more gypsum
1 ounce Saaz or Cascade hops (boil)
1/4 ounce same type hops (finishing)
1/4 ounce same type hops (dry hops)
1 teaspoon Irish moss
1 packet lager yeast
1 1/4 cups corn sugar (priming)

• Original gravity: 1.050

Brewer's specifics

Grind the malt and prepare the brewing water. Wash the rice and boil in 6 quarts mash water until gelatinized (about 45 minutes). Add to remaining 3 quarts mash water, along with 1 1/2 teaspoons gypsum.

Bring mash water to 125 degrees F and stir in malt. Protein rest 118-125 degrees F for 45 minutes. Boost to 155 degrees F in 20 minutes. Starch conversion rest 150-155 degrees F for 45 minutes. Boost to 168 degrees F and rest 5 minutes. During mash, check temperature and stir frequently. Always stir when applying heat.

Transfer mash to lauter tub, heat sparge water to 160 degrees F and sparge.

Add more gypsum (if needed) to boiler and boil wort 1 1/2 hours. After 1/2 hour add boiling hops; 15 minutes before end, add Irish moss. At end of boil, turn off heat, stir in finishing hops, and rest 1 hour.

Strain wort into primary, removing one quart for starter. Top up to 5 gallons if necessary, cover and force cool. Meanwhile, force cool starter wort to 80 degrees F and add yeast.

When wort is cool (70 degrees F) stir up starter and pitch it in. Ferment in a cool place (50-55 degrees F ideally). When fermentation slows down (SG approximately 17) put dry hops in bottom of secondary and rack. Fit airlock. When fermentation is over (no gravity drop for 5 days) terminal gravity should be 11-13. Rack into primary, add priming sugar and bottle. Age 2 to 3 months.

Recipe from David G. Miller's *Homebrewing for Americans*, published by Amateur Winemakers Publications Ltd., England.

Esslingen
Todd Hanson
Sheyboygan, Wisconsin
First Place, Export, 1987
(all-grain recipe)

Ingredients for 10 gallons
  18 pounds Schreier 2-row pale malt
  2/3 pound caramel malt — 40 degrees Lovibond

2/3 pound wheat malt
1/2 pound dextrine malt
  2 teaspoons gypsum
1/2 teaspoon salt
3/4 ounce Northern Brewer hops (90 minutes)
1/4 ounce Hallertauer hops (90 minutes)
1/2 ounce Hallertauer hops (60 minutes)
1/4 ounce Northern Brewer hops (60 minutes)
3/4 ounce Hallertauer hops (30 minutes)
1/4 ounce Tettnanger hops (30 minutes)
1/2 ounce Hallertauer hops (after boil)
1/8 ounce Cascade hops (after boil)
     Semplex lager yeast, pure culture
     CO_2 pressure to prime, sterile filtered

- Original specific gravity: 1.050
- Terminal specific gravity: 1.020
- Age when judged (since bottling): 2 months

Brewer's specifics

   Mash: protein rest at 122 degrees F for 45 minutes. Boost to 153 degrees F in 11 minutes. Rest at 153 to 155 degrees F for 75 minutes. Boost to 170 degrees F in 10 minutes.

MUNICH/
MÜNCHENER

Munich/Münchener. A bottom-fermented beer produced in the Bavarian city of Munich since the mid-19th century. The original Münchener was dark. In 1928, the Paulaner Brewery introduced a paler version, called Helles, that has almost entirely overtaken the darker brew. Both versions, helles Bier (or Munich pale lager) and dunkel Bier (or Munich dark lager), are lightly hopped (180 to 200 grams per hectoliter) and distinctively malty because Munich malt is used. Both have an alcohol content of about 3.5 to 4.0

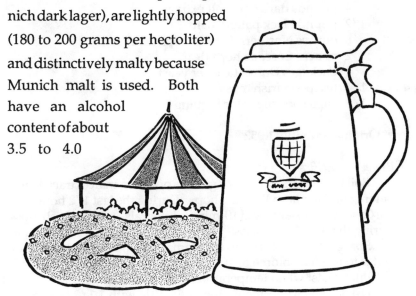

percent by weight (4.4 to 5.0 percent by volume). Munich-style beers brewed outside Germany are always dark.

Kulmbacher

Tony Green
San Jose, California
First Place, Munich Dunkel, 1982
(extract recipe)

Ingredients for 10 gallons
      11 pounds light dry malt extract
       4 pounds dark dry malt extract
   1/2 pound black patent malt
       6 ounces Northern Brewer hops (leaf)
       2 ounces Cascade hops (leaf)
       2 packages Domestic lager yeast
   1/4 teaspoon Irish moss
1 1/2 cups corn sugar for bottling

• Original gravity: 1.052

Brewer's specifics
      Boil for 3 hours with 2 1/2 gallons of water, malt extract, black patent and Northern Brewers hops. During the last 1/2 hour add the Cascade hops evenly at 10-minute intervals. Add the Irish moss during the final 10 minutes.
      Sparge the hot wort into the primary fermenter and add cold water to reach a volume of 10 gallons.
      Pitch yeast when temperature is about 72 degrees F.
      Use secondary fermentation and bottle with 1 1/2 cups corn sugar.

Continental Gold

Gary Bauer
Milwaukee, Wisconsin
First Place, Munich Helles, 1985
(all-grain recipe)

Ingredients for 5 gallons
6 pounds 6-row malt
3 pounds Munich malt
1/2 pound Cara-Crystal (dextrine) malt
1/2 pound wheat malt
1/2 ounce Hallertauer (10 percent) hop pellets (1 hour)
1/4 ounce Tettnanger (10 percent) hop pellets (35 minutes)
1/4 ounce Tettnanger hops (15 minutes)
No. 308 (home cultured) lager yeast
CO_2 pressure for carbonation

- Original specific gravity: 1.050
- Terminal specific gravity: 1.012
- Double-stage fermentation in glass at 38 degrees F for 3 weeks
- Age when judged (since bottling): 6 weeks

Judges' comments
"Beautiful color and clarity. Sweet malty aroma. Delicious, clean flavor; highly drinkable, reminds me of Paulaner Urtyp."

Helles

Dave Miller
St. Louis, Missouri
First Place, Munich, 1987
(all-grain recipe)

Ingredients for 6 gallons
8 pounds 2-row pale lager malt
1 ounce Hallertauer hops (60 minutes)
1 ounce Hallertauer hops (30 minutes)

1/2 ounce Hallertauer hops (15 minutes)
 40 milliliter foil packet "Brewer's Choice" liquid lager
      yeast
  1 cup dextrose to prime

- Original specific gravity: 1.046
- Terminal specific gravity: 1.012
- Age when judged (since bottling): 3 1/2 months

Judges' comments
    "I really liked this aroma and was surprised it led to as thin-bodied a taste as it did. Very nice job on the appearance of this beer. Flavor is quite thin. Needs more malty sweetness for this category. More akin to a light lager of American origin. A cleanly brewed beer. Good technique...free from defects."
    "Aroma OK, would like to feel a more hearty malt and hop nose come through. Appearance outstanding in all respects. The flavor is delicately balanced — often difficult to achieve in lighter brews. A little more pronunciation of the malt and hops needed. Excellent brew and extremely drinkable. It is mellow and light without any harshness."

Sweetwater Lager
Byron Burch
Santa Rosa, California
First Place, Munich, 1988
(all-grain recipe)

Ingredients for 10 gallons
    16 pounds Klages malt
     2 pounds Vienna malt
   3/4 pound Munich malt
     6 ounces caramel-90 malt
     1 ounce Tettnanger hop pellets (60 minutes)
     2 ounces Tettnanger hop pellets (30 minutes)
     1 ounce Hallertauer hop pellets (dry hopped)

2 tablespoons Irish moss (unground flakes)
1/8 teaspoon calcium carbonate
30 milliliters No. 308 liquid lager yeast
   forced CO_2 to prime

- Original specific gravity: 1.048
- Terminal specific gravity: unknown
- Age when judged (since bottling): 2 months

Judges' comments
   "Nice hop aroma, delicate. I pick up DMS (dimethyl sulfide), winelike. Boil longer. Cool more quickly. Nice pale color, very clear, good bubbles. Can taste DMS too. Very, very clean. Excellent. A bit hoppy. Could use more malt sweetness by cutting back on hops 10 to 15 percent, not a serious problem. No faults other than DMS in aroma and a tad bitter."
   "Slight aroma of malt and hop, no off-aromas. Copper colored, clear, nice head, looks great. A lot of residual sweetness, no off-flavors, a little thin bodied. A very clean, well-made brew. Perhaps a bit sweet. I enjoyed it."

PILSENER

Continental Pilsener.
A general name for pale, golden-hued, highly hopped bottom-fermented beers. The original Pilsener was first brewed at the Bürgerlisches Brauhaus in the Bohemian town of Plzen (meaning green meadow) in Czechoslovakia in 1842. It was then the palest beer available and a style that was soon copied worldwide. The archetypal Pilsener is presently known as Plzensky Prazdroj or Pilsner Urquell (Urquell means "original source"). The name was patented in 1898.

This type of beer is brewed with very soft, almost mineral-free water from an original wort gravity of 1.048 (12 degrees Balling) for an alcohol content of 4 percent by weight (5 percent by volume). It is highly hopped with local Saaz hops at a rate of 400 to 500 grams per hectoliter (as opposed to 200 to 220 grams per hectoliter for Dortmunder).

American Pilsener. The typical use of adjuncts such as corn and rice in combination with a clean fermentation contributes to an uncomplicated, crisp brew with a universal lightness of body and flavor. American Pilseners are aggressively carbonated, but not overcarbonated.

Dutch Light Lager

Dennis Crawford
Casper, Wyoming
First Place, European Light Lager, 1986
(Continental Pilsener)
(mash-extract recipe)

Ingredients for 5 gallons

3 1/3 pounds Laaglander Dutch light lager hopped malt extract syrup
5 1/2 cups Munton & Fison light dry malt extract
8 ounces crystal malt
1/2 ounce Hallertauer hop pellets (1 hour — added after wort had boiled 15 minutes)
1/2 ounce Hallertauer hop pellets (30 minutes)
1 teaspoon non-iodized table salt
2 packages Red Star lager yeast
1 cup corn sugar to prime

- Original specific gravity: 1.046
- Terminal specific gravity: 1.012
- Age when judged (since bottling): 2 months

Judges' comments

"Appearance is perfect for category. Nice subtle hop aroma. No off-aromas detectable. Needs a higher specific gravity — add dextrine. Not enough fullness, body too thin, needs more malt. If you used brewing salts, maybe cut them out; the aftertaste is salty. Addition of malto-dextrine could easily correct lack of body."

"Very nice-looking beer. Nice head and beading. Very nicely balanced malt/hop aroma. Very good-tasting beer, has slight salty taste, nicely balanced. Could use slightly more crispness that cold fermentation should give."

"Gold appearance. Bouquet has a nice balance. Hops just muted enough. Slight salt flavor, sweet. Seems like a decent beer. Flavors could be blended more by colder fermentation and cold lagering."

Light-Bodied Light Lager

Donald F. Thompson
Dallas, Texas
First Place, Light-bodied Light Lager, 1982
(Continental Pilsener)
(all-grain recipe)

Ingredients for 5 gallons

    7   pounds 2-row malted barley
1 1/2   ounces Cascade hops
        tap water
        "Paul's Lager Yeast" (brewery yeast for cold
        fermentation)
  3/4   cup corn sugar

• Original specific gravity: 1.042

Brewer's specifics

Step infusion mash: "Mash-in" with two gallons of water at 126 degrees F and hold for 30 minutes. Raise temperature to 144 degrees F and hold for 30 minutes. Raise temperature to 158 degrees F and hold for 1 1/2 hours.

Sparge with 160 degrees F water until wort runs out at 1.010.

Bring wort to boil for one hour and 20 minutes. Add all hops for the last 60 minutes of boiling.

Sparge wort through spent hop "filter bed" (hop-back).

Cool wort to 61 degrees F and pitch active yeast starter. Main fermentation to be carried out at about 54 degrees F.

When fermentation is complete, prime the beer with about the equivalent of 3/4 cup corn sugar, then bottle.

OWBC UR-PILS

Gary Bauer
Milwaukee, Wisconsin
First Place, Classic Pilsener, 1985
(Continental Pilsener)
(all-grain recipe)

Ingredients for 5 gallons

    6 pounds six-row barley malt
    2 pounds dark Munich malt
  1/2 pound wheat malt
  1/2 pound Cara-pils malt
  1/2 ounce Saaz hops (boil 1 1/4 hour)
  1/2 ounce Saaz hops (boil 1 hour)
    1 ounce Saaz hops (boil 3/4 hour)
  1/2 ounce Saaz hops (boil 1/4 hour)
  1/4 ounce Saaz hops dry hopped in secondary
    4 ounces Weisenheimer No. 308 liquid lager yeast

- Original specific gravity: 1.050
- Terminal specific gravity: 1.014
- Fermentation temperature: 50 degrees F in primary, 40 degrees in secondary
- Age when judged (since bottling): 2 weeks

Brewer's specifics

Mash at 158 degrees F for 1 1/2 hours. Sparge with water at 174 degrees to collect 6 gallons.

Judges' comments

"Appearance is crystal clear — 'fire of life,' but too dark, and large bubbles. The aroma has a good balance but lacks some of the 'burnt' malt aroma of Pilsener Urquell. Good balance and body, no fermentation defects — less intense than the standard. A very fine brew — please send me the recipe or better yet, a case!"

"Outstanding clarity, by far the best here, but too dark for the category. The bouquet is delightful! Ooh-la-la! The malt is just the right intensity. (I wish I knew how you did it. A different malt character than the standard, but heck — how are you going to get Czechoslovakian malt in the United States?) Aroma better than flavor as a harshness marred the flavor."

Pillowtalk Pilsener

Byron Burch
Santa Rosa, California
First Place, Pilsener, 1988
(Continental Pilsener)
(all-grain recipe)

Ingredients for 10 gallons

     14   pounds Klages malt
 1 1/2   pounds Munich malt
      6   ounces crystal malt
      2   ounces Tettnanger hop pellets (60 minutes)
      2   ounces Tettnanger hop pellets (30 minutes)
      2   ounces Hallertauer hop pellets (30 minutes)
      4   ounces Hallertauer hop pellets (10 minutes)
  1/4   teaspoon gypsum
  1/4   teaspoon salt
      2   tablespoons Irish moss
    30   milliliters No. 308 liquid lager yeast
 1 1/2   cups corn sugar to prime

- Original specific gravity: 1.046
- Terminal specific gravity: unknown
- Age when judged (since bottling): 5 1/2 months

Brewer's specifics
Mash all grains at 150 degrees F for 1 hour. Sparge with 165 degree F water.

Judges' comments
"Malty with good hop aroma. Great, dark yellow color. Almost too gushy, but head holds up. Light and balanced. Export type. Very good balance. Very fresh, clean finish. Great beer."
"Slight vegetable odor then hops come through. Slight haze. Good head retention. Nice balance struck here. I enjoy the finish. Samuel Adams Lager?"

Pilsener

David Guillebeau
Tuscaloosa, Alabama
First Place, All-Grain Light, 1983
(Continental Pilsener)
(all-grain recipe)

Ingredients for 5 gallons
     9 pounds lager malt
   2/3 pound Munich malt
   1/4 pound crystal malt
3 1/4 ounces Saaz hops
     1 teaspoon calcium chloride
     2 teaspoons table salt
   1/2 teaspoon citric acid
     1 teaspoon Irish moss
   1/4 cup Polyclar
     1 package Milwaukee lager yeast
   3/4 cup corn sugar
     8 gallons distilled water

- Original specific gravity: 1.048
- Terminal specific gravity: 1.012
- Approximate temperature of fermentation: 50 to 55 degrees F
- Age when entered (since bottling): 5 months

Brewer's specifics

Bring 2 1/2 gallons water to 136 degrees F. Add minerals and citric acid. Add that to the grain in a cooler prepared for mashing.

After 30 minutes scoop out some of the mash and add it to 1 gallon of water. Bring that to a boil and return to the mash.

Keep mash at 158 to 160 degrees for 30 minutes. Sparge to 6 gallons.

Boil this for 15 minutes, then add 2 ounces hops. At 45 minutes add 1 ounce hops, and at 1 1/2 hours add 1 teaspoon Irish moss.

At the 2-hour mark remove from heat. Wait 1 hour then strain through cheesecloth and add water to make 6 gallons. Cool and add yeast.

When gravity reaches 1.015, rack to secondary adding 1/4 ounce hops and Polyclar. Prime and bottle 8 weeks.

Judges' comments

"Hoppy aroma, hoppy flavor."
"A bit over-hopped — good beer."
"Hoppy, well balanced."

Aster Pils

DeWayne L. Saxton
Chico, California
First Place, American Pilsener, 1985
(extract recipe)

Ingredients for 20 gallons

- 6 pounds Munton and Fison light malt extract
- 6 pounds Munton and Fison light dry malt extract
- 1/2 pound wheat malt
- 9 pounds corn sugar
- 1/4 pound Cascade pellet hops (1 hour)
- 1/8 pound Brewers Gold leaf hops (1 hour)
- 1/4 pound raw Cascade hops (30 minutes)
  distilled water
- 1/2 teaspoon citric acid

    3 teaspoons non-iodized rock salt
1/2 teaspoon gypsum
    3 teaspoons crystal yeast nutrient in 1/4 cup dry extract
    4 packets Muntona ale yeast
    5 cups corn sugar to prime

- Original specific gravity: 1.034
- Terminal specific gravity: not available
- Age when judged (since bottling): 2 months

Brewer's specifics
    Add corn sugar at the end of the wort boil. Ferment in secondary for 1 1/2 months.

Judges' comments
    "Brilliant color with a slight chill haze; good initial head. A subtle aroma but balanced, fine for the category. Good flavor balance and body, but a slightly sour and mildly bitter aftertaste, possibly due to oxidation and/or sugar."

Hammer's

Todd Hanson
Sheboygan, Wisconsin
First Place, American Pilsener, 1984
(all-grain recipe)

Ingredients for 5 gallons
    5 pounds Schreier's two-row "Michelob" malt
1/2 pound Briess Munich malt
1/2 pound Briess pale six-row malt
    1 pound rice
1/2 pound corn grits
3/4 ounce Hallertauer hops (boil 30 minutes)
1/4 ounce Hallertauer hops (boil 5 minutes)
1/4 ounce Hallertauer dry hopped in secondary
    2 teaspoons gypsum
    1 package Semplex beer yeast

- Original specific gravity: 1.028
- Terminal specific gravity: 1.007
- Fermentation temperature: 50 to 55 degrees F
- Age when judged (since bottling): 10 weeks

Brewer's specifics
Mash times (1 3/4 hours total): 45 minute protein rest at 120 to 125 degrees F. Boost to 155 within 25 minutes. Starch conversion at 155 for 20 minutes. Boost to 168 and hold for 5 minutes. Carbonated in a pre-mix tank at 50 psi for 36 hours at 35 degrees F after the lagering in CO_2-purged gallon jugs.

Judges' comments
"Good golden color, good clarity, good balance. Flavor is a little thin but otherwise a good effort!"
"Well brewed for appearance. Malt overpowers the aroma and flavor balance."
"Excellent clarity and color; good flavor balance."
"Nice golden color. Distinct metallic aftertaste—the brewpot? Good carbonation."

Pilsener

Gary Bauer
Milwaukee, Wisconsin
First Place, American Pilsener, 1985
(all-grain recipe)

Ingredients for 5 gallons
    6 1/2 pounds 6-row malted barley
    2/5 pound Munich malt
    1/3 pound Cara-Pils (dextrine) malt
    1/2 ounce Tettnanger (10 percent) pellet hops (75 minutes)
    1/4 ounce Tettnanger pellets (30 minutes)
    1/4 ounce Tettnanger pellets (10 minutes)
        No. 308 (home cultured) lager yeast
        CO_2 pressure for carbonation

- Original specific gravity: 1.040
- Terminal specific gravity: 1.008
- Double-stage glass fermentation at 38 degrees F for 3 weeks
- Age when judged (since bottling): 8 weeks

Judges' comments

"Aroma has a beautiful balance with prominent malt and compensating hoppiness. Definite diacetyl — nice, but out of character; otherwise, very clean. Flavor has a very good balance, with hops really coming through at finish and lingering aftertaste — perhaps a bit strong and overbodied for the category. A great brew, only slightly out of character for the category."

"Superb sparkle, like a commercial beer, and no yeast sediment. Nice full, grainy malt aroma with hops lightly in the background. Hop bitterness seems a bit strong for the category, but it is an expertly made beer."

RAUCHBIER

Rauchbier. In Germany, a dark, bottom-fermented beer produced by a few breweries in the city of Bamberg in northern Bavaria.

Its unique roasted or smoked flavor is produced by using malts dried over an open fire of moist beechwood logs. According to some researchers, this technique dates back to 1678.

Lazy Rauch
Alan Lee, George Ashley, Bob Zahray
Bryan, Texas
First Place, Rauch, 1987
(all grain)

Ingredients for 5 gallons
9 pounds Munton & Fison lager malt
2 ounces Hallertauer (60 minutes)
No. 308 yeast starter
3/4 cup sucrose to prime

* Original specific gravity: 1.055
* Terminal specific gravity: 1.008
* Age when judged (since bottling): 1 1/2 months

Brewer's specifics
Spread 9 pounds of malt on window screeen and place on barbecue grill at one end of large pit over wood fire with flames at the other end of the pit. Allow to smoke no more than 10-15 minutes. Continue brewing as usual.

Judges' comments
"There is a light smoke aroma. Very light in color. Moderate smoke flavor, reasonable balance, with a smoky aftertaste combined with a hop finish. A very enjoyable brew with good balance."

"I would like this to have a smokier aroma. The head is beautiful, small bubbles. Great tight, well balanced brew with more smoke quality than I was expecting."

Rauchbier
P.L. Dillon
Arlington, Texas
First Place, Specialty Beer, 1985
(all-grain recipe)

Ingredients for 6 gallons
9 pounds home-smoked Klages malt

  1 pound Munich malt
  1/2 pound dark caramel malt
  1 3/4 ounces Hallertauer hops (1 hour)
  1/4 ounce Hallertauer hops (dry hop)
      bottom-fermenting yeast culture

- Original specific gravity: 1.048
- Terminal specific gravity: 1.016
- Double-stage fermentation in plastic and glass at 30 to 48 degrees F for 6 weeks.
- Age when judged (since bottling): 4 weeks

Brewer's specifics
  Mash at 122 degrees F for 30 minutes; 144 degrees F for 30 minutes; 158 degrees F for 60 minutes; 170 degrees F for 10 minutes.

Judges' comments
  "Exquisite color and crystal clear. Definitely has the smoky aroma and flavor that it's meant to."

  "Head is a bit flat but clarity and color are superb! Looks like a fine, tawny port. No problems with the flavor. Would be an excellent beer with barbeque or smoked salmon and cheese."

  "Gorgeous color and clarity. Hickory smoke aroma. Smoke beer has not been my favorite but I do like this. Excellent for appetizers or cheese."

Untitled

Todd Hanson
Sheboygan, Wisconsin
Third Place, Rauch, 1987
(all-grain recipe)

Ingredients for 5 gallons
  8 pounds 2-row pale Klages malt
  2 pounds smoked 2-row pale malt
  1 pound corn grits
  5 ounces wheat malt

2 1/2   ounces caramel 40 lovibond malt
   1   ounce chocolate malt
 3/16   ounce Perle hops (90 minutes)
  1/8   ounce Northern Brewer hops (90 minutes)
 1/16   ounce Perle hops (60 minutes)
 3/16   ounce Saaz hops (60 minutes)
 1/16   ounce Perle hops (30 minutes)
 1/16   ounce Saaz hops (30 minutes)
 1/16   ounce Tettnanger hops (30 minutes)
  1/8   ounce Perle hops (1 minute)
 1/16   ounce Saaz hops (1 minute)
   1   package Semplex beer yeast
      polish-filtered and CO_2 pressure added for carbonation

- Original specific gravity: 1.056
- Terminal specific gravity: 1.014
- Age when judged (since bottling): 1 month

Brewer's specifics

Steep 2 pounds of 2-row malt in 125 degree F water, then smoke in a home smoker until the malt crystalizes (about 12 hours).

Mash grains at 122 degrees F for 45 minutes. Boost to 155 degrees F for 16 minutes. Rest at 155 degrees F for 45 minutes. Boost to 170 degrees F for 8 minutes.

Judges' comments

"Very light smoke aroma is present. Clear, dark amber in color. Light carbonation. A clean well balanced brew, with only very minimal smoke flavor, minimal aftertaste. An enjoyable brew, but the smoke flavor may be too subtle."

"This has a very subtle smoke quality. If I hadn't known it was a rauch beer, I might not have picked it out. Exquisite color and lovely head. The smoke comes through better in the flavor. This is a nice well-balanced brew. Subtle enough to drink in quantity without being overwhelmed. Good job."

STEAM BEER

American Steam Beer.
A beer produced by hybrid
fermentation using bottom yeast fermented at top yeast temperatures (15 to 20 degrees C, 60 to 70 degrees F). Fermentation is carried out in long, shallow pan-like vessels called
clarifiers followed by warm-conditioning at 10 to 12 degrees C (50 to 55 degrees F) and kraeusening. This style of
beer is indigenous to America and was first produced in California at the end of the 19th century (during the Gold Rush)

where temperatures were too warm for proper fermentation of bottom yeasts.

At one time there were as many as 27 breweries making steam beer in San Francisco. It is presently brewed by the Anchor Steam Brewing Company under the registered trademark name of Steam Beer. No brewery may use this term for commercial reasons. This is a highly hopped, amber-colored, foamy beer containing 3.8 percent alcohol by weight (4.74 percent by volume). This beer style is named after the hissing sound produced when a cask is tapped and pressure released.

Entenbrau Hell

Mike Fertsch
Woburn, Massachusetts
First Place, Steam, 1987
(extract recipe)

Ingredients for 5 gallons
- 3 1/3 pounds Bierkeller light malt extract syrup
- 2 1/2 pounds light dry malt extract
- 1/4 pound crystal malt
- 1/2 pound malto-dextrin
- 1 1/2 ounces Hallertauer pellet hops (60 minutes)
- 1/2 ounce Hallertauer pellet hops (30 minutes)
- 1/2 ounce Cascade leaf hops (1 minute)
- 1 package Bierkeller yeast
- 3/4 cup dextrose to prime

- Original specific gravity: 1.047
- Terminal specific gravity: 1.016
- Age when judged (since bottling): unknown

Judges' comments
    "Nice clean aroma, perhaps too clean. Good color and head, slightly cloudy, flavor is clean. Lacks full-bodied character of

steam. This beer is too clean tasting. Tastes like it was lagered, lacks the complex character of a warm ferment. Otherwise a very tasty, well balanced steam beer."

"Good nose, I guess Hallertauer hops. Good color, nice head retention, clean. Good all-around flavor. Very drinkable brew. I like it. Hop/malt blend is okay. Basically a superb beer."

"Clean hops, but slightly off in aroma. Malt is a hair too subdued. Slight chill haze, but a beautiful color. Malt taste is too clean and hops should be Northern Brewer. Anchor has a little sweetness that this lacks. Best so far this evening. A very nice blending — very tasty. Could use better clarity."

No. 39

Glen Mazur
Buffalo Grove, Illinois
First Place, Steam Beer, 1988
(mash/extract recipe)

Ingredients for 5 gallons
4	pounds 2 row pale ale malt
3	pounds light dry malt extract
1	pound crystal malt
1 1/2	ounces Eroica hops (boil)
1/2	ounce Cascade hops (finish)
1/4	ounce Cascade hops (dry hop)
	Wyeast U.S. Lager liquid yeast
3/4	cup dextrose to prime

- Original specific gravity: 1.046
- Terminal specific gravity: 1.010
- Age when judged (since bottling): 4 months

Brewer's specifics
All grains mashed at 155 degrees F for 1 1/2 hours.

Judges' comments
"Nice, clean, hoppy, appetizing aroma. Slight haze, but very

nice color, carbonation and head. Clean flavor with a distinctive strong hop bitterness finish true to style. This is a very good representation of the steam category, a job well done."

"Distinctly hoppy aroma. Full rich bouquet. Clear amber brew. Good conditioning, fair head retention. Crisp initial taste balanced by a hoppy finish. A very good, appropriate example of this uniquely American beer."

Untitled
Michael Janicki
Aurora, Colorado
First Place, American Steam Beer, 1983
(mash/extract recipe)

Ingredients for 5 gallons
    3 1/3 pounds John Bull light extract
    1 pound lager malt grain
    6 ounces crystal grain

Bittering hops:
    1/2 ounce Cascade
    1/2 ounce Hallertauer
    1/4 ounce Bullion

Finishing hops:
    3/4 ounce Cascade
    1/2 ounce Hallertauer
    1/2 ounce Willamettes
    1/2 ounce Tettnanger

    1 teaspoon salt
    1 1/2 teaspoons gypsum
    3 teaspoons Sparkolloid
    1 package Danish lager yeast
    1 teaspoon yeast energizer (secondary)
    1 1/4 cups corn sugar for priming

- Original specific gravity: 1.042
- Terminal specific gravity: 1.005
- Approximate temperature of fermentation: 62 degrees F
- Age when entered (since bottling): 8 weeks

Brewer's specifics
Modified mashing at 155 to 158 degrees F with 1 pound lager malt grain and 6 ounces crystal grain.

For 1 hour, boil 2 gallons of water with the extract, mashing liquor, salt, gypsum and Sparkolloid. Fifteen minutes after the boil begins, add 1/2 ounce Cascade and 1/2 ounce Hallertauer hops. Thirty minutes after boil begins add 1/4 ounce Bullion hops. Sparge to make 5 gallons. Pitch yeast at 72 degrees F.

Leave bag of finishing hops in primary for 3 days. Have the bag large enough for the wort to flow easily through the hops. Rack to secondary and add 1 teaspoon yeast energizer. Bottle with corn sugar after 12 days in the secondary.

Judges' comments
"Very good beer. Bouquet/aroma a little malty. Slightly dry for category. No other complaints. Good work!"

"This beer is great! However, we are looking for a maltier body," not so hoppy and dry. Boy, I like it."

"Good hops. Dry. Well-made brew."

Morgan's Touch Amber
Scotty Morgan
San Jose, California
First Place, American Steam Beer, 1985
(all-grain recipe)

Ingredients for 11 1/2 gallons
   20 pounds Canadian pale malted barley
    3 pounds Canadian crystal malt
    1 ounce Northern Brewer hops (70 minutes)
    1 ounce Tettnanger hops (50 minutes)

  1 ounce Tettnanger hops (30 minutes)
  1/2 ounce Northern Brewer hops (10 minutes)
  1/2 ounce Northern Brewer hops (end of boil)
  domestic lager yeast
  1 cup corn sugar to prime

- Original specific gravity: 1.048
- Terminal specific gravity: 1.014
- Double-stage fermentation; first in stainless, then glass at 60 to 64 degrees F for 3 weeks.
- Age when judged (since bottling): 2 months

Brewer's specifics
   Mash the grains at 158 degrees F for 1 hour; sparge for 45 minutes with 170 degree F water; cool and pitch yeast at 65 degrees F.

Judges' comments
   "Good color, similar to the standard. Nice bouquet but short on maltiness and needs more sweet malt flavor. The yeast did not compact well."
   "Excellent color; a little low on carbonation. Very smooth, well balanced and aged flavor. Tastes almost exactly like Anchor Steam. Great job!"

Untitled

Nancy Vineyard
Santa Rosa, California
First Place, All-Grain Light Beer, American Steam, 1983
(all-grain recipe)

Ingredients for 5 gallons
  9 1/2 pounds U.S. pale malted barley
  1 1/2 pounds U.S. crystal malted barley
  1 3/4 ounces Northern Brewer hop pellets (for bittering)
  1 ounce Cascade hop pellets (aromatic)

2 teaspoons gypsum
1 teaspoon non-iodized salt
2 packages Red Star lager yeast

- Original specific gravity: 1.042
- Terminal specific gravity: 1.007
- Age when entered (after bottling): 6 months
- Approximate temperature of fermentation: 58 to 63 degrees F

Brewer's specifics

Three-step infusion mashing: mash 15 minutes at 95 degrees F to pH 4.8; 30 minutes at 125 degrees F; and 1 1/2 hours at 148 degrees F.

Use 1 1/2 quarts water per pound of grain-mashing liquor. Add gypsum and salt. Transfer to a picnic cooler fitted with a copper strainer coil. (Or set up your own sparging system.)

Heat 4 gallons of water to 175 degrees F for sparging and run off in 15 minutes to collect 6 gallons.

Boil with Northern Brewer hops. Add 1 ounce of hops at beginning of boil. After 45 minutes add remaining 3/4 ounce and continue to boil for 20 minutes. Add the Cascade hops during the final 3 minutes of boiling. Strain hops by siphon transfer from boiler to primary. Cool wort and pitch yeast.

Judges' comments

"Nice taste balance; good carbonation; nice bouquet. I like this beer!"

"Great beer — would you send me a recipe? Very hoppy! Maybe a little more malt taste could balance it more."

"Could use more malt with slightly more caramel. Body a little light and carbonation low."

VIENNA

Vienna Lager. An amber-colored, bottom-fermented beer originally brewed in Austria where it has become rare. This beer is now called Spezial to differentiate it from the classic version. Vienna-style lagers, still brewed in South America and Mexico, are amber-colored, lightly hopped, malty and fairly strong (4.4 percent alcohol by weight or 5.5 percent by volume).

Oktoberfest. A bottom-fermented Vienna- or Märzen-style beer originally brewed especially for the Oktoberfest but now available year round. Oktoberfest beer, brewed from an original wort gravity of 1.050 to 1.060 (12.5 to 15.0 degrees Balling) is copper-colored, malty and sweet.

Märzen (bier). In Germany, before the advent of artificial refrigeration, beer was brewed in winter. The last batch, brewed in March, was made especially strong to survive the many months of maturation before it was drunk at the end of the summer.

Märzen is a Vienna-style, bottom-fermented blond beer. It was invented in 1871 by Josef Sedlmayr, owner of the Zum Franziskanerkeller, to contrast with the brown beers then popular in Bavaria. The first batch was brewed in March 1872, hence the name March beer, and was served for the first time at the Oktoberfest of that year. Today's Märzenbiers, still a favorite of the Oktoberfest, contain about 4.5 percent alcohol by weight (as opposed to 3.5 to 3.9 percent for ordinary pale beers called *helles*) and are fermented at an original wort gravity of 12.5 to 13.0 degrees Balling.

Because of the similarities in style of the two beers, the terms Vienna and Märzen are sometimes used interchangeably.

Old Stock Amber

George Fix
Arlington, Texas
First Place, Vienna, 1987
(all grain)

Ingredients for 10 gallons

   18 pounds 2-row malt
    1 pound Cara-pils (dextrin) malt
    1 pound amber malt
  1/2 pound black patent malt
    2 ounces sodium chloride
    3 ounces Hallertauer hops (30 minutes)
    3 ounces Saaz hops (15 minutes)

commercial (Pittsburgh Brewing) yeast
20 percent kraeusen—fresh wort to prime

- Original specific gravity: 1.055
- Terminal specific gravity: 1.014
- Age when judged (since bottling): 1 1/2 months

Brewer's specifics
Mash at 135 degrees F for 30 minutes, 152 degrees F for 30 minutes, 165 degrees F for 5 minutes. Sparge at 165 degrees F.

Judges' comments
"Good maltiness, caramel-like aromas. Excellent head retention. Good clarity. Excellent amber color. Nice initial sweetness. Good amount of malt. Good balance. Very good. Keep it up!"

"Very nice aroma, rich and malty. Good head retention, excellent color and clarity. Malty flavor, but not quite enough hops. A very nice beer but just a bit too sweet."

Humpback Lager

John C. Maier
Juneau, Alaska
First Place, Vienna, 1988
(all-grain recipe)

Ingredients for 5 gallons
6 pounds pale Klages malt
3 pounds Munich malt
3/4 pound Cara-pils malt
1/2 pound crystal malt (40 degrees Lovibond)
1 ounce Hallertauer hops (60 minutes)
1/2 ounce Hallertauer hops (10 minutes)
1/2 ounce Hallertauer hops (after boil)
1/4 teaspoon Yeastex
1 package Wyeast American Lager liquid yeast
3/4 cup dextrose to prime

- Original specific gravity: 1.052
- Terminal specific gravity: 1.012
- Age when judged (since bottling): 7 1/2 months

Brewer's specifics
    Mash all grains at 120 degrees F for 30 minutes. Infuse boiling water to raise temperature to 153 degrees F for 15 minutes. Apply heat and raise temperature to 170 degrees F. Sparge with 170 degree F water. Collect 6 gallons sweet wort.

Judges' comments
    "Slightly malty aroma, fairly bland, no hop character. Nice orange-copper color. Very clear, good head. Nice malt start with a clean hop finish. Lacks character and body. A very well-balanced beer, but a little thin and bland. Consider using more Vienna malt to increase body and character. No off-flavors."
    "Subtle hop aroma comes through, could be a bit maltier in aroma. Bright very clear, fine bead. Nice bitter aftertaste, just the right amount of hops, well balanced with malt. Could use just a bit more body. Add some crystal or Cara-pils. Could use more malt for style. Hops linger and this style should have more maltiness."

Dortmunder Light
Robert Schafer
Portland, Oregon
First place, Oktoberfest, 1986
(extract recipe)

Ingredients for 5 gallons
    6 2/3 pounds Hansberg Dortmunder light malt extract syrup
    1/2 ounce Saaz and 1/2 ounce Hallertauer pellets (60 minutes)
    1/2 ounce Hallertauer pellets (last minute)
    1/2 teaspoon Irish moss (added 30 minutes into boil)
    2 packages Red Star lager yeast
    3/4 cup corn sugar to prime

- Original specific gravity: 1.049
- Terminal specific gravity: 1.010
- Age when judged (since bottling): 2 months

Judges' comments
"Mild clean aroma, faintly hoppy. Lacks malt nose. Great product—I can drink this all day. Not quite assertive enough. Your technique is fine. Minor recipe changes will produce a winner, not that this isn't; be proud!"

"Good aroma balance. Just a bit shy on hops. Seemed almost stale — too old? Oxygen in the bottling?"

"Perfect color and clarity! Beautiful small-bubble, creamy head. Nice delicate toasted malt flavor and very clean. Nice job!"

Han's Ale
Russell Schehrer
Boulder, Colorado
Second Place, Oktoberfest, 1985
(extract recipe)

Ingredients for 6 gallons
6 2/3 pounds John Bull light malt extract
2 ounces Northern Brewer hops (40 minutes)
1 ounce Cascade hops (last minute)
Irish moss
Munton and Fison beer yeast
1/2 cup corn sugar to prime

- Original specific gravity: 1.048
- Terminal specific gravity: 1.018
- Age when judged (since bottling): 6 1/2 months

Judges' comments
"Beautiful appearance, great job here! Big malt and floral hop aroma. Surprisingly good flavor; a bit thin on body and sweetness for the bitterness."

Maerzen 53

Jason Schumaker
Vancouver, Washington
First Place, Oktoberfest, 1985
(mash/extract recipe)

Ingredients for 4 1/2 gallons
    3 1/2 pounds Edme light malt extract
    1 1/2 pounds dry dark malt extract
        1 pound Munich malt
        1 pound dextrin malt
      1/2 pound flaked barley
        1 ounce Cascade hops (1 hour)
      2/3 ounce Cascade hops (30 minutes)
      1/2 ounce Saaz hops (15 minutes)
      1/4 ounce Saaz hops (at end)
        2 teaspoons gypsum
      3/4 teaspoon table salt (sodium chloride)
      1/4 teaspoon Epsom salt (magnesium sulfate)
        2 packets Red Star dry lager yeast
      1/2 teaspoon corn sugar per bottle to prime

- Original specific gravity: 1.048
- Terminal specific gravity: 1.013
- Age when judged (since bottling): 5 months

Brewer's specifics
    Mash the syrup and malts at 142 degrees F for 30 minutes, bring up to 158 degrees F for 1 hour. Sparge with water at 170 degrees F.

Judges' comments
    "Bountiful color, brilliant. Ample body with just a hint of a fruity-spice flavor."
    "Aroma has a slight ester—nice, but could use a bit more hop character. Flavor is a tad bit bitter for Oktoberfest; cut back on the hops 20 percent. Nice job. Cleanly brewed, the only drawback is excessive bitterness, but is a good Octoberfest."
    "Looks beautiful. Slight apple flavor is very nice but perhaps not appropriate."

Vienna

Gary Bauer
Milwaukee, Wisconsin
First Place, Oktoberfest, Maerzen Beer,
Vienna Style Lager, 1985
(all-grain recipe)

Ingredients for 5 gallons

6 1/2	pounds 6-row malt, preground
2	pounds Munich malt, preground
1/2	pound Cara-Crystal (dextrine) malt, preground
1/2	ounce Hallertauer (10 percent) hop pellets (1 hour)
1/4	ounce Hallertauer hops (40 minutes)
1/4	ounce Hallertauer hops (15 minutes)
	No. 308 (home cultured) lager yeast
	CO_2 pressure for carbonation

- Original specific gravity: 1.050
- Terminal specific gravity: 1.012
- Double-stage fermentation in glass at 38 degrees F for 4 weeks
- Age when judged (since bottling): 3 1/2 weeks

Brewer's specifics

Mash grains at 156 degrees F for 1 1/2 hours.

(Editor's note: I think Gary has a real good thing going with that No. 308 lager yeast as well as his brewing technique. He has taken first place in the American Pilsener, European Lager and Oktoberfest all-grain categories.)

Judges' comments

"Great job on appearance. Beautiful aroma; a nice bit of butterlike diacetyl lends itself to malt. I suspect this is a ringer! Wonderful stuff, professional quality. A bit high in diacetyl, but class A+ brew."

"Beautiful brew; nice deep amber to light auburn color; decent head retention. Malty floral smoothness in the aroma — suggests richness. Lovely brew, slight hit of fruity-spice flavor. I can hear the polka music!"

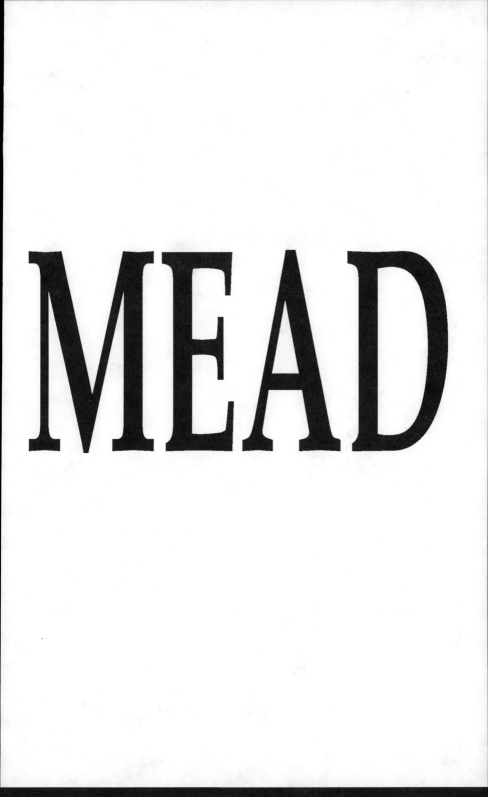

MEAD

MEAD

Mead. An alcoholic beverage produced by fermenting honey and water. Mead can be dry, sweet or sparkling.

Cyser. A variety of melomel prepared by fermenting a must of honey, apple juice and water.

Melomel. Any mead in which part of the honey has been replaced by crushed fruits or fruit juices. Syn: fruit mead.

Metheglin. Any mead flavored with herbs

and spices. Etym: From the Welsh words medclydlin and med-dyglyn meaning medicine.

Pyment. A variety of melomel prepared by fermenting a must of honey, grapes or raisin juice and water. Sometimes spelled: pymeat.

Mi'apa Sparkling Mead
Jim Saunders
Boulder, Colorado
First Place, Mead, 1980
(Traditional)

Recipe for 5 gallons
Boil for 1 hour:
   1 1/2 gallons water
     7 pounds clover or alfalfa honey
     2 pounds corn sugar
     1 ounce Fuggles hops
   1/4 teaspoon Irish moss
   1 1/2 teaspoon gypsum
     1 teaspoon citric acid
   3 1/2 ounces freshly-grated gingerroot
     3 tablespoons whole cloves
     3 sticks cinnamon

Steep for an additional half hour:
   1 1/2 ounces freshly grated gingerroot

• Age when judged (since bottling): 11 months

Brewer's specifics
    After gingerroot has steeped, sparge. Add water. Add 2 1/2 teaspoons yeast nutrient and 1 package of beer yeast. Add 1 cup corn sugar when bottling.

Festival Cyser

Wayne Waananen
Denver, Colorado
Second Place, Mead, 1988
(Cyser)

Ingredients for 5 gallons
12 pounds wildflower honey
4 gallons apple cider
4 teaspoons acid blend
2 packets Red Star champagne yeast
5 teaspoons yeast nutrient

* Original specific gravity: 1.102
* Terminal specific gravity: .993
* Age when judged (since bottling): 16 months

Judges' comments
"Apple aroma comes through nicely. Beautiful appearance. Well done, good balance of flavor. Really nice, appropriate character for cyser. Well done. Very cleanly brewed."

"Aroma very appley, fruity, slightly alcoholic with some honey characteristics. Golden color, very clear. Good appley flavor and finish, thin to medium body, dry finish, good balance of alcohol and acidity. A little bit of astringency on finish. Good apples, good balance, good mead."

Black Raspberry Mead

Bill Pfeiffer
Wyandotte, Michigan
First Place, Sparkling Meads, 1985
(Melomel)

Ingredients for 4 gallons
6 pounds honey
19 ounces Vine-Pro black raspberry concentrate

10 teaspoons acid blend
1/2 teaspoon grape tannin
1 package all-purpose wine yeast
1/2 cup malto-dextrin, 1/2 cup corn sugar and 2 cups
lactose to prime

- Original specific gravity: 1.062
- Terminal specific gravity: 0.990
- Age when judged (since bottling): 8 months

Judges' comments
"Tart flavor, maybe a bit young. Great mouth feel, pleasant fruity aroma and a clean taste."
"Real nice color, flavor and body."

Morat
Ralph Bucca
District Heights, Maryland
First Place, Mead, 1988
(Melomel)

Ingredients for 1 gallon
3 pounds mulberries
1 1/2 pounds honey
1 1/2 pounds dextrose
1 teaspoon acid blend
1 package Red Star wine yeast
3 tablespoons honey to prime

- Original specific gravity: 1.085
- Terminal specific gravity: 1.010
- Age when judged (since bottling): 15 months

Brewer's specifics
The mulberries were crushed and added to 1 gallon hot water and stirred. Then the honey and corn sugar were added. When

cool, the yeast and acid blend were added. After one week the must was strained off the fruit and racked to a secondary fermenter. The mead was racked three more times. When bottled, 3 tablespoons honey were added for carbonation.

Judges' comments
"Pleasant honey-berry aroma. Dark, brownish port coloring. Vinous, like an oxidized chardonnay. Alcoholic. This stuff will knock you back! Interesting floral, estery bouquet. Very pleasant after-dinner drink. A bit oxidized but lacking in off-flavors and nicely balanced in sweetness, acidity, body and carbonation."

"Complex delightful aroma. Winelike appearance. Could use a tad more tannin. Gusher. Overcarbonated and somewhat sweet residual finish. Surprising pronounced vinous quality. Somewhat oxidized in color and taste, not unpleasant, like a well-aged wine. Could have done without the carbonation. Would make a lovely red-port style wine. A fine remarkably winelike product. Makes me want to run out and find a mulberry tree!"

Blueberry Ginger Mead
Mervin (Brad) Kraus
Houston, Texas
Third-place, Mead, 1987
(Melomel/Metheglin)

Ingredients for 5 gallons
    8 1/2 pounds West Texas mesquite honey
       6   pounds crushed blueberries
       3   ounces grated ginger root
     1/2   ounce Comet whole hops
       3   teaspoons Super Ferment yeast nutrient
    1 1/2 teaspoons gypsum
       1   package Red Star Champagne yeast
     1/4   pound pasteurized honey
     1/2   pound dewberries in two cups water to prime

- Original specific gravity: 1.058
- Terminal specific gravity: 0.995
- Age when judged (since bottling): 1 year 8 months

Judges' comments
   "Aroma is wonderful! Appearance beautiful! A kept promise
— tastes as good and clean as I anticipated from the aroma and
color. This is an exquisite mead!"
   "Smells good.   I can't wait to taste this!   Lovely color and
clarity! Although tarter than I like meads, this has excellent flavor.
Lovely to behold and kind to the palate."

Mike's Birthday Mead
Mike Kunetka
Aurora, Colorado
Second Place, Sparkling Meads, 1985
(Melomel/Metheglin)

Ingredients for 5 gallons
     9 pounds honey
    10 pounds cherries
     1 pound fresh mint
     1 ounce Cascade hops (1 hour)
 1 1/2 teaspoons gypsum
     1 package Edme ale yeast
     4 teaspoons yeast nutrient
     1 cup corn sugar to prime

- Original specific gravity: 1.060
- Terminal specific gravity: 1.008
- Age when judged (since bottling): 9 months

Brewer's specifics
   After honey and hop boil, steep mint and cherries for 20
minutes in hot wort. Then dilute and ferment entire contents. No
sparging.

Judges' comments
"Bright color, distinctive fruity aroma and flavor and clean aftertaste. This is fun to drink!"
"Lovely color and flavor. Where's the mint?"

Raspberry Lemongrass Ginger Mead

Robert Townley
Westminster, Colorado
First Place, Sparkling Mead, 1983
(Melomel/Metheglin)

Ingredients for 18 gallons
  25 pounds honey
   3 ounces Cascade hop pellets
   4 ounces grated ginger root
 1/2 teaspoon citric acid
   6 teaspoons yeast nutrient
 80 ounces frozen raspberries
    Champagne yeast
1 1/2 ounces dried lemongrass
2 3/4 cups priming sugar

- Original specific gravity: 1.058
- Terminal specific gravity: 0.994
- Approximate temperature of fermentation: 70 degrees F
- Age when entered (since bottling): 6 months

Brewer's specifics
Boil for 1 hour: the water, honey, hops, ginger root and Irish moss. Sparge into the primary and add to the warm wort: corn sugar, citric acid, yeast nutrients and the raspberries. Add water to make 18 gallons. Pitch the yeast at 70 to 78 degrees F.

After 1 week, skim the raspberries off the top and rack into the secondary. Steep the lemongrass in a small pot of boiled water and carefully strain through a fine sieve and cheesecloth. Add this to the mead in the secondary.

Bottle with priming sugar after 3 weeks or when fermentation is complete.

Judges' comments
"Smooth, fruity flavor; clear delicate color; lively aroma. Highly drinkable — good for all night!"
"Love the aroma; nice sweetness."

Still Dewberry Mead
Jana Cezeaux
Bryan, Texas
First Place, Still Meads, 1984
(Melomel/Metheglin)

Ingredients for 5 gallons
 7 pounds honey
 5 pounds dewberries
 3 ounces ginger root
 1 ounce Willamette leaf hops
1 1/2 teaspoons gypsum
      Champagne yeast
 5 teaspoons diammonium phosphate yeast nutrient

- Original specific gravity: 1.060
- Terminal specific gravity: .990
- Age when judged (since bottling): 5 months

Brewer's specifics
Sweetened with non-fermentable sugar. Bulk aged for 5 months.

Judges' comments
"Pleasantly dry, good body, fruity taste. Easy to drink."
"Very nice and dry; great body!"

Barkshack Gingermead No. 12

Roger Haynes
Thousand Oaks, California
First Place, Mead, 1981
(Metheglin)

Ingredients for 5 gallons
    5 pounds citrus/sage honey
    2 ounces cut and dried ginger root
    2 pounds corn sugar
  1/4 teaspoon Irish moss
    1 teaspoon acid blend
    2 teaspoons gypsum
    3 teaspoons yeast nutrient (2 for primary, 1 for secondary)
1 1/4 ounces Hallertauer hops (pellets)
      water to make total of 5 gallons
    1 package Vierka light lager yeast

Brewer's specifics
    Boil 1 hour with 2 gallons of water all of the above ingredients except yeast, Irish moss and yeast nutrient. During the last 10 minutes of the boil add the Irish moss.
    Sparge this concentrated wort by passing the liquid through a strainer into a primary fermenter. Rinse the catch with 3 gallons of cold water.
    When temperature has dropped to 75 degrees F, add yeast and yeast nutrient as called for in recipe. Ferment in primary until gravity drops to 1.015-1.020 or no longer than a week. Ferment in a 5-gallon glass secondary for at least one month or until fermentation is complete.
    To bottle, rack, then add 1 cup corn sugar, dissolve well, bottle and cap. Age for 8 months or more. Barkshack Gingermead begins to reach its prime after 12 months in the bottle.
    This is a 9 percent alcohol, dry, light, bubbly champagne mead with a refreshing hop and ginger sparkle.

Riesling Pyment 64D

John M. Montgomery
Bryan, Texas
First Place, Sparkling Mead, 1986
(Pyment)

Ingredients for 6 3/4 gallons
- 14 pounds Brazos Valley Apiaries' dark honey
- 4 pounds Alexander's Sun Country Emerald Riesling grape concentrate
- 3 tablespoons acid blend
- 2 tablespoons pectic enzyme
- 1 package Champagne yeast
- 1 package Montrachet yeast mixed with 1 pint Welch's white grape juice to prime

- Original specific gravity: 1.098
- Terminal specific gravity: 1.008
- Age when judged (since bottling): 3 1/2 months

Judges' comments
Grape smell is really wonderful. This is a really tasty mead. Congratulations! I really think you're on your way. No off-flavors evident to my taste buds.

Cabernet Pyment No. 43

John Montgomery
Bryan, Texas
First Place, Still Meads, 1985
(Pyment)

Ingredients for 1 1/2 gallons
- 2 3/4 pounds dark honey
- 11 1/2 ounces red grape juice concentrate
- 5 grams Montrachet wine yeast

- Original specific gravity: 1.077
- Terminal specific gravity: not available
- Age when judged (since bottling): 5 months

Judges' comments
    "Nice earthy aroma, winelike, not expected in a mead. Seems slightly carbonated at first."
    "Earthy flavor, clean aftertaste."

Index by Brewer

Examine the World of Microbrewing and Pubbrewing

Travel the world of commercial, small-scale brewing; the realm of microbrewers and pub-brewers.

The New Brewer magazine guides you through this new industry. Its pages introduce you to marketing, finance, operations, equipment, recipes, interviews—in short, the whole landscape.

Subscribe to *The New Brewer* and become a seasoned traveler.

HOMEBREWER?

Get The Whole Story!

ZYMURGY

Vol. 16 No.1 Spring 1993 Published by the American Homebrewers Association $5.00

For Every Season, There Is A Beer
Track Your pH
Grasp the Basics of Chemistry
AHA 1993 Conference Insert
10 Beer Recipes

Join the thousands of American Homebrewers Association members who read **zymurgy** — the magazine for homebrewers and beer lovers.

Every issue of **zymurgy** is full of tips, techniques, new recipes, new products, equipment and ingredient reviews, beer news, technical articles — the whole world of homebrewing. PLUS, the AHA brings members the National Homebrewers Conference, the National Homebrew Competition, the Beer Judge Certification Program, the Homebrew Club Network, periodic discounts on books from Brewers Publications and much much more.

Mail this coupon today and join the AHA or call now for credit card orders, (303) 447-0816.

Name

Address

City   State/Province

Zip/Postal Code   Country

Phone

☐ Enclosed is $29 for one full year.
Canadian memberships are $34 US, Foreign memberships are $44 US.

☐ Please charge my credit card ☐ Visa ☐ MC

Card No.   Exp. Date

Signature

Make check to: American Homebrewers Association, PO Box 1510, Boulder, CO 80306 USA
Offer valid until 12/31/94.   Prices subject to change.   Code :SABP

BOOKS for Brewers and Beer Lovers

Order Now ... Your Brew Will Thank You!

These books offered by Brewers Publications are some of the most sought after reference tools for homebrewers and professional brewers alike. Filled with tips, techniques, recipes and history, these books will help you expand your brewing horizons. Let the world's foremost brewers help you as you brew. So whatever your brewing level or interest, Brewers Publications has the information necessary for you to brew the best beer in the world — your beer.

Please send me more free information on the following: (check all that apply)

◇ Merchandise & Book Catalog
◇ American Homebrewers Association
◇ Institute for Brewing Studies
◇ Great American Beer Festival

Ship to:

Name

Address

City   State/Province

Zip/Postal Code   Country

Daytime Phone   (   )

Payment Method

◇ Check or Money Order Enclosed (Payable to the Association of Brewers)
◇ Visa   ◇ MasterCard

Card Number   Expiration Date

Name on Card   Signature

Brewers Publications, PO Box 1679, Boulder, CO 80306-1679, (303) 447-0816, FAX (303) 447-2825.

BP-O93

BREWERS PUBLICATIONS ORDER FORM

PROFESSIONAL BREWING BOOKS

QTY.	TITLE	STOCK #	PRICE	EXT. PRICE
_____	Brewery Planner	440	80.00	_____
_____	North American Brewers Resource Directory	445	80.00	_____
_____	Principles of Brewing Science	415	29.95	_____

THE BREWERY OPERATIONS SERIES
from Micro and Pubbrewers Conferences

QTY.	TITLE	STOCK #	PRICE	EXT. PRICE
_____	Volume 4, 1987 Conference	424	25.95	_____
_____	Volume 5, 1988 Conference	428	25.95	_____
_____	Volume 6, 1989 Conference	430	25.95	_____
_____	Volume 7, 1990 Conference	433	25.95	_____
_____	Volume 8, 1991 Conference, Brewing Under Adversity	442	25.95	_____
_____	Volume 9, 1992 Conference, Quality Brewing — Share the Experience	447	25.95	_____

CLASSIC BEER STYLE SERIES

QTY.	TITLE	STOCK #	PRICE	EXT. PRICE
_____	Pale Ale	431	11.95	_____
_____	Continental Pilsener	434	11.95	_____
_____	Lambic	437	11.95	_____
_____	Vienna, Märzen, Oktoberfest	444	11.95	_____
_____	Porter	443	11.95	_____
_____	Belgian Ale	446	11.95	_____
_____	German Wheat Beer	448	11.95	_____
_____	Scotch Ale	449	11.95	_____
_____	Bock (available Winter 1993)	452	11.95	_____

BEER AND BREWING SERIES, for homebrewers and beer enthusiasts
from National Homebrewers Conferences

QTY.	TITLE	STOCK #	PRICE	EXT. PRICE
_____	Volume 8, 1988 Conference	427	21.95	_____
_____	Volume 9, 1989 Conference	429	21.95	_____
_____	Volume 10, 1990 Conference	432	21.95	_____
_____	Volume 11, 1991 Conference, Brew Free Or Die!	435	21.95	_____
_____	Volume 12, 1992 Conference, Just Brew It!	436	21.95	_____

GENERAL BEER AND BREWING INFORMATION

QTY.	TITLE	STOCK #	PRICE	EXT. PRICE
_____	Brewing Lager Beer	417	14.95	_____
_____	Brewing Mead	418	11.95	_____
_____	Dictionary of Beer and Brewing	414	19.95	_____
_____	Evaluating Beer	456	25.95	_____
_____	Great American Beer Cookbook	455	24.95	_____
_____	Winners Circle	407	11.95	_____

Call or write for a free *Beer Enthusiast* catalog today.
• U.S. funds only.
• All Brewers Publications books come with a money-back guarantee.
*Postage & Handling: $3 for the first book ordered, plus $1 for each book thereafter. Canadian and foreign orders please add $4 for the first book and $2 for each book thereafter. Orders cannot be shipped without appropriate P&H.

SUBTOTAL _____
Colo. Residents Add
3% Sales Tax _____
P & H * _____
TOTAL _____

Brewers Publications, PO Box 1679, Boulder, CO 80306-1679, (303) 447-0816, FAX (303) 447-2825.